Can You Just Get Them Through Until Christmas?

The Turnaround Story of One Lay Minister and Two Small, Rural Churches

Pastor Margie Briggs

Cass Community Publishing House

For more information and further discussion, visit
ccpublishinghouse.org

Cover art and design by
Rick Nease
www.RickNeaseArt.com

Published by Cass Community Publishing House
Copyediting and layout by Front Edge Publishing, LLC.

For information about customized editions, bulk purchases or
permissions, contact Cass Community Publishing House at
11745 Rosa Parks, Detroit, MI 48206 or
ffowler@casscommunity.org.

To Anna E. Nave Lutjen, daughter of a circuit riding preacher and granna to a granddaughter who gives thanks each day for the life lessons she gave to me.

Contents

Introduction

Once upon a time, there were two small, rural congregations that were in trouble. One church was located in a Missouri town with a population of about 450 people and the other one was situated roughly five miles away on a gravel road, seven and a half miles outside of a second town. The average combined Sunday morning worship attendance at the Calhoun and Drake's Chapel United Methodist Churches had dropped to fourteen and, to make matters worse, they didn't have a pastor. This book chronicles my assignment to these churches in crisis, and an emergency or two of my own.

This is not the story of a suburban theologian converging onto the scene and doing some sort of cutting-edge ministry that develops into a megachurch attracting thousands of people in a short period of time. No, this book describes a decade-long journey together. It involves a second-career lay minister—whose only degree was in life—and her Midwestern parishioners, who decided to do ministry, mission and outreach together with the unchurched and de-churched people in their towns.

It is important to underscore that every journey involves setbacks. This was true for our time together, as well. Some people left the churches. At one point, some ugly rumors were started about what was happening. Still, it is equally true that perseverance, prayer and the involvement of laity transformed two fledgling congregations into viable and vibrant communities of faith with frequent baptisms and new members, youth activities and mission experiences. Calhoun and Drake's Chapel are still small and rural, but they are making disciples and making a difference today proving that a church doesn't have to be large to have a large impact.

It is my hope that the stories in this book will rekindle the fire of people who have lost faith in churches that have fewer than 100 members. There is an urgent need for small churches both in declining rural areas and in impersonal metropolitan areas where many struggle with isolation and loneliness. Small churches don't need to create a system of small groups to help people fit in; they are natural places of intimacy. The key is to use that closeness to greet new and different people.

I likewise hope that readers will be inspired to better involve lay people. Their gifts and graces are ripe for the picking. John Wesley put them to work inside and outside the Foundry. Methodism began as a lay movement and, I believe, the ministry of the laity is crucial to its future. This includes utilizing certified lay ministers, many of whom come from rural communities and want to remain in them. One of the biggest self-esteem hurdles for small churches is the revolving door installed for clergymen and clergywomen who stay just long enough to start climbing the "ladder" to what are deemed bigger, better and more prestigious appointments.

To dive deep, I highly recommend that you use Kay Kotan's Study Guide as you read the book. It contains a list of Key Concepts and Reflection Questions for each chapter. You can use the Study Guide as an outline if you want to journal after each chapter or it would serve as an excellent springboard if you are going to facilitate small group sessions. The Study

Guide will help you apply what you have learned from the stories in your local setting. It will also open up the opportunity for congregational conversations and reflections. Our prayer is that by working through the Study Guide (personally and/or collectively), your congregation will move into action that provides a more effective and fruitful ministry.

May God use and bless you as you envision a turnaround of your own.

—*Margie Briggs*
   March 2017

Chapter 1

TWENTY-TWO YEARS. AFTER 22 years, you come to believe that things are secure and predictable, but there would be no anniversary party for me. I started working when my husband, Dick, was on strike from General Motors, and for four years, I was the administrative assistant to the city administrator in Harrisonville, Missouri.

Then I took a position at Times-Mirror Microwave in 1985. It was also located in Harrionsville, Missouri, and was 17 miles from my house. The company changed its name four times during my tenure, but my role as a field-ops administrator remained the same: The job involved assisting eight technicians from Terre Haute, Indiana to Gainsville, Texas. I was responsible for receiving and processing broken equipment, preparing spreadsheets and analyzing data for my manager.

In 1996, I made a major find. The company was paying to repair a defective part that was still under warranty by another firm. The discovery saved our business over $750,000, and so the company flew my husband and me to a black-tie dinner at an impressive country club in Texas. They gave me a huge inscribed marble award that night, along with a $1,000 bonus.

In 2000, the company—then Broadwing Communications—relocated to downtown Kansas City. The long drive, mostly in rush-hour traffic, was grueling. What choice did I have, though? The building was in the Jazz District. Ours was a brand-new office, complete with a kitchen for the staff. My desk was right by the front door. Given the high crime rate in the area, the exterior doors had bulletproof glass. Soon after the move, though, my manager took a job at the corporate headquarters, in Austin, Texas. I received a new manager: Harold. Harold was relatively young for his position, and maybe that was why he wanted everyone to understand that he was in charge.

I arrived one Tuesday morning and Harold was already at work, which was unusual. He summoned me to his office and put a Human Resources representative on speakerphone. I knew what was coming next. Reorganization meant that many of my colleagues had already disappeared. I listened to the matter-of-fact voice: "Your job is being eliminated. We'll give you two weeks' severance pay … " I was stung by the callousness, but I was also determined not to break down.

When I returned to my desk, it was surrounded by empty banker boxes. The manager and a technician stood guard, even though they couldn't look at me. I felt like a thief. There was quite a bit to scoop up—22 years of pictures, notes from colleagues and trinkets from vacations. My computer had been locked so that I couldn't even tell friends across the country what had happened or say goodbye. I stopped at the staff kitchen to pick up my coffee cup and dishes.

I loaded the cartons with my belongings into the trunk of my car, and drove away. I didn't make it all the way home, though—actually, I drove down the street and had to pull into a Salvation Army parking lot, where I cried my heart out.

"Oh, God, what am I going to do now?"

Chapter 2

MARK WAS IN his late 30s when he got the call. Until that point, he had lived and worked in Kansas City, selling insurance. After that pivotal phone call, Mark traded his lucrative, commission-based salary for that of a local pastor and attended a License to Preach School before being assigned by the district superintendent—a United Methodist minister in charge of supervising all of the churches and pastors in a geographic area. Mark's district superintendent sent him to serve two small congregations in rural Missouri.

The Calhoun and Drake's Chapel church buildings were a relatively short distance apart, and on Sunday mornings, Mark left the parsonage early, eager to serve the Lord and both congregations. Although there were very few children or young adults in either congregation, it didn't lessen his joy in shepherding the people.

Mark's mother was an ordained minister in the United Methodist Church. She had been on staff at the multi-site Church of the Resurrection in Kansas before she retired. Mark inherited some of her congeniality, as well as her natural talent as a speaker. The parishioners at both churches loved that he always began his sermons with a joke. His flock also appreciated that Mark lived in the parsonage and related to people in the neighborhood. He visited the post office and talked with the employees at the city hall practically every morning.

Mark's Sundays began with services at Calhoun. The church's sanctuary was in need of repair: several of the clear window panes were broken, and covered with thick Styrofoam to keep the cold and the insects out. Dirty white drapes hung over the grey Styrofoam. The pews were curved to fit the rounded architecture, and a couple of choir members without robes sat on the elevated area near the altar—as did the piano player.

The accompanist, Linda Alford, started playing shortly before the Call to Worship at 9:30 a.m. Prayers, hymns, Scripture readings, the sermon and benediction all needed to be over within an hour, because Mark had to drive East 52 to get to Drake's Chapel and prepare for the 11 a.m. service there. The building dates back to 1853, when it had a Circuit Rider—a minister who traveled, usually on horseback, to more than one congregation each week. The Drake's Chapel floor plan had a main aisle down the center of the sanctuary, flanked by rows of straight, wooden pews. Each pew had a golden-hued seat cushion, to make the worshippers feel comfortable. There was an organ at Drake's Chapel, but the piano was the instrument of preference.

Directly across the dirt road was the church's cemetery. It was immaculate. On Memorial Day, every veteran's tombstone was decorated with a small American flag and all of the graves were adorned with flowers. An old tree had died in the cemetery recently, and an artist from Jefferson City had carved an angel out of its trunk. The cherub stands tall with a cross behind her extended wings, and her weathered, wooden face seems watchful. Visitors often remark that she resembles a pensive Native American woman.

Mark played cards with some of the men from church. Two of them from Calhoun, Tom and Jim, grew close with the local pastor in a relatively short period of time. Tom had been born and raised in the area. A history buff, he spent hours on the road, researching local lore. Tom had been employed by the cheese factory in the county seat of Clinton before taking a job at the armory. He had married a local girl, and they had become members of the Calhoun church in the early months of their 50-year marriage. The new pastor learned quickly that Tom was someone who could be counted on to make the necessary repairs at the church.

Tom's friend Jim was also a good worker. Jim was a "Joseph" kind of man—without fanfare, he quietly took care of manual tasks. He changed the church's light bulbs, arranged tables for church dinners and kept the steps and walkways clear of snow for Sunday worship. Jim held and protected the church mail until it could be handed off to the pastor. At 5 feet 7 inches tall, Jim was bald-headed and had an infectious smile. He courted his second wife—Verna, a widow—on her porch swing, and together they raised her three children and his three. They have been together for more than 25 years.

On a Sunday morning in April, Tom and Jim were concerned that Mark hadn't arrived at church by 9:15. He was normally punctual. Tom mentioned seeing the pastor's pickup truck under the carport in his driveway. Maybe he was finishing up extra chores at the parsonage since, as they also knew, Mark's brother was coming down from Kansas City to spend the afternoon with him. Five minutes. Ten minutes. Finally, the duo decided to check on him.

The house on Olive Street was just three blocks away. The drive didn't take them any time at all. They knocked on the front door. There was no answer, and so they let themselves in, since the entrance wasn't locked. Mark's body was on the couch in the front room. A 12-gauge shotgun was positioned between his legs with its muzzle resting on the edge of the sofa. A copy of Mark's will rested on a seat next to his body. Mark was lifeless. Jim called the police to report Mark's apparent suicide. Tom returned to the church to inform the congregation.

A handful of parishioners were still sitting in the pews. Tom revealed that their pastor was dead. He asked Bob, another congregational leader, to offer a prayer for Mark and his family. At Drake's Chapel, after an identical announcement, the congregation lingered at the church until both of Mark's brothers arrived. They shared the tragic news with them, and then Mark's siblings drove to the parsonage. Tom and Jim, along with Mark's brothers, waited on the lawn with a police officer who was stationed outside the house. They watched silently, like the angel in the Drake's Chapel cemetery, as Mark's body was removed from the parsonage by staff members of Hadley's Funeral Home.

A funeral service for Mark took place at the Calhoun church on Wednesday, May 4. His body was laid out in an unusual casket: Mark had kidded his friends that he was going to be buried in a purple casket that he had purchased on a road trip. The following day, a second funeral occurred in Grandview, using a more traditional casket. His body was then laid to rest in a Kansas City cemetery.

Chapter 3

IN TIMES OF tragedy or adversity, I am most grateful for the "connectional" nature of the United Methodist Church. Every congregation is related to all of the other congregations. Every local church belongs to a district, an annual conference, a jurisdiction and the General Conference. Each of these groups is larger than the previous—a district tends to involve less than 100 churches; an annual conference, hundreds of churches; a jurisdiction, thousands of them; and, finally, the General Conference includes all of the United Methodist churches worldwide. These relationships create a safety net, which becomes conspicuous whenever there is a natural disaster or a crisis brought about by people. The district superintendent, Rev. Cody Collier, brought in reinforcements immediately after learning about Mark's death. Denominational leaders filled the pulpit and helped hold the congregations together in the months following their pastor's funeral.

In August, the district superintendent called me. I had known Cody since he arrived in Missouri from Mississippi in 1984. He was a man short in statue but full of grace. Cody put you at ease. He helped you believe that you were worthy. He had the ability to make you feel safe enough to express yourself without any fear of judgment. When Cody—a good friend for nearly 30 years—asked me if I would preach at Calhoun and Drake's Chapel every other Sunday until he could identify a permanent replacement, how could I have said no to him?

The only other person in my life whom I could never refuse was my grandmother, "Granna." My mother deserted our family when I was just 3 years old, and soon thereafter, my father, my older brother and I moved into my grandparents' home on Florence Street in Windsor, Missouri. It was a modest dwelling. There was a coal chute on the side of the house that went directly into the basement, and the back porch served as the entrance to the downstairs. It also held the wringer washing machine. Granna pulled that washing machine into the kitchen every Monday to do laundry. The clean, wet clothing hung out to dry on the backyard clothesline.

Granna sang as she did the laundry, "Jesus, Jesus, Jesus, the sweetest name I know." To say she was religious was like commenting that she was heavyset with bobbed hair and always clad in an apron. It was a matter of fact. She never said as much, but I suspected that my grandmother's faith took even deeper roots when my father was stricken with polio. He was only 7 years old when the muscles in his legs were attacked. Granna's large, rough hands gently rubbed his legs for hours at a time, praying that he wouldn't lose his ability to walk. My whole life, my father was confined to a wheelchair or stabilized by crutches.

Granna's father had been a circuit rider for the Methodist Church in Benton County, Missouri. Each Sunday, I took her hand as we walked to the Methodist church on Main Street in Windsor. Attendance was expected. So was giving. There was a Mason jar on the round, oak table in the dining room. It didn't contain green beans like the ones in the cellar; it held nickels. Every time we received nickels as part of our change, the rule was that we had to contribute them to the Mason jar. Granna used the coins to pay her pledge to the WSCS, the Women's Society of Christian Service. This giving was always above her pledge to the church.

When I had young children of my own, we continued the tradition of keeping a Mason jar. Every time it was full of nickels, the family would gather to decide where the money should be donated. To this day, I smile when 5-cent pieces are a part of my change. Not long ago, a cashier apologized because she was out of dimes and only had one quarter in her drawer. "I hope you don't mind nickels," she half-apologized.

"Not at all," I replied.

I was baptized in Granna's church. I held a perfect attendance record for Sunday school that spanned 15 years. I belonged to the youth group and sang in the chancel choir. I married my husband, Dick, at the altar while I was a senior in high school—just before he left to serve in Taiwan during the Vietnam War.

Once I was an adult, I took the training class required to become a lay speaker. This allowed me to assume leadership roles in my congregation and to assist with worship. I served as a lay leader for 10 years before completing the classes necessary to become a certified lay speaker. The certification meant that I could go to other churches to fill in as "pulpit supply" when members of the clergy were away. It also resulted in groups like the United Methodist Women inviting me to speak at other churches and neighboring pastors asking me to talk at potluck dinners during Lent and Advent. Mostly, my presentations had the goal of raising money to help electrify a mission hospital in Zimbabwe.

"Could you love them through this?" Cody asked again.

"I'll try," I answered.

Chapter 4

I WASN'T USED to putting together a different sermon every other week. It took me five hours of preparation—reading, writing and practicing the messages—before my sermons were ready for their Sunday debut. In a way, though, preaching didn't feel that much different from delivering my mission presentations at area churches. What felt out of the ordinary was that the parishioners were still numb from the tragic loss of Mark.

They talked about him nonstop, as if it would bring him back to life or settle their secret battles. They reminisced about his involvement in the community, his leadership during worship and his winning personality. They described him affectionately, as a gregarious and jovial man. They must have commented a thousand times that "It Is Well with My Soul" was his favorite hymn. It had been mine, too.

What went unspoken for them were the questions left unanswered. How could a man of God take his own life? Why hadn't they recognized any signs that he had needed help?

Hadn't he known how much they loved him and needed him? Hadn't he known how much his suicide would hurt them? Could they even go on as a Church? One husband and wife left the Calhoun Church before I even arrived. They told people that God had condemned the pastor to hell. Suicide, they ranted, was an unforgivable sin. The couple never returned.

Another Calhoun congregant had lost her husband to suicide not long before Pastor Mark died. She arranged for counselors to be available at both churches. She knew first-hand the cruel judgment that survivors must endure. She understood that some questions don't have answers. She concluded that pastors aren't immune to problems. Whatever caused Mark to feel trapped, she wanted to make sure that members of his churches weren't overtaken by unresolved anger or grief.

For two months, I preached about God's love and grace. I listened to anyone who was ready to talk. Then, in October, Cody let me go. He had found a licensed local pastor to serve the churches quarter-time. This was good news for the churches. A licensed local pastor can officiate during Holy Communion and baptisms where he or she is appointed. As a lay minister, I always had to ask a clergyperson to be present to officiate when the sacraments were celebrated in "my" churches. Yet I was both relieved and disappointed at being dismissed. It reminded me of the times Dick and I cared for foster children: pouring love into them and yet knowing the whole time that we would need to pass them on to other parents. The letting go is an act of love and it is hard.

Amazingly, volunteers from both churches had torn up the blood-soaked parsonage carpet and replaced it. They had scrubbed the walls and painted them so that the parsonage was in pristine condition before the new minister moved in. I am unsure whether or not the people at Calhoun and Drake's Chapel were, themselves, ready for a new minister. The mourning process was taking a lot longer than I had expected.

Many people in both congregations were critical of the new pastor's leadership. If the parsonage porch light was on, he told them it meant, "Do not disturb." They said that it was always lit. When the minister and his wife attended the annual conference meeting, which required several days away from home, they ran up what the churches' members considered excessive bills for lodging and food. The straw that broke the camel's back, though, was the episode when the pastor was a bell ringer for the Salvation Army in Clinton. At the end of his shift, he took the collection bucket home. On Sunday morning, police officers were waiting for him outside the church. I don't know if charges were filed, but the pastor left shortly after. His time at the churches had only been a year.

Cody called me, a little panicked. "Can you just get them through until Christmas?" he asked.

"Of course," I responded without hesitation.

Archie – Debbie Arvelo (FE) (1)

Atherton - Paul Bond (RE) (5)

**Bethel (Hughesville)/Blackwater Chapel -
Wes Wingfield (PL) (1)**

Brandon - John Streit (SY) (5)

Buckner - Linda Wansing (PL) (3)

Calhoun/Drake's Chapel - Margie Briggs (CL) (11)

**Centennial (Kansas City) – Jason Bryles (PE) (1)
Associate – Jeffrey Williams (PL) (1)**

Central - Trevor Dancer (FE) (2)

Chilhowee - Susan A. Smith (PL) (9)

Christ – Mike Costanzo (FE) (1)

Church of the Resurrection (Blue Springs) - Penny
Ellwood (FL) (7)

Clinton - Brad Reed (FE) (3)

Chapter 5

AFTER CHRISTMAS, WHILE I was serving on the Commission on the Status and Role of Women (COSROW), I had the opportunity to attend a two-week seminar in New York. COSROW does advocacy work with and for women with the intention of eliminating inequalities in the United Methodist Church and in the world. The topic for the conference I attended was human trafficking. It was intense and eye-opening. Linda Bales Todd was my roommate. We had just returned from a session at the United Nations when Cody called once more.

I ducked into the bathroom in order to hear better. "Margie," he said, "I have talked to Drake and Calhoun and they want you to stay."

"I really don't want them to give up the chance to have a pastor who can baptize or consecrate the elements," I answered. It was the time of the year when churches could request a new pastor, and I was sure that they would want someone who had full rights to provide the sacraments. Maybe the two churches could afford a part-time pastor.

The district superintendent assured me, though, that the churches did not care about those things. "They want you," he said.

I told Cody that I would pray about it and call him back.

"I don't know if I'm good enough," I told Linda later.

"They think you are," she replied, "and with God's help, you will be."

I remember thinking: *Could I write a sermon every week?* It had been hard enough when I thought I only had to prepare sermons until Cody appointed someone else.

I flew home and talked to Dick. "Cody called," I told him nonchalantly. "Calhoun and Drake want me to take over: to be their pastor."

He smiled and said, "Well, it's what you've always wanted to do."

I must have given him a puzzled look.

"I have always known that you felt a calling. … You would have been doing it a long time ago if it wasn't for me," he continued.

He was probably right. He wouldn't have wanted to be a pastor's spouse, but now I was 58 and he was 61 and it didn't seem so far-fetched. Dick's only request was that the rest of the family remain at the Creighton church. "They need me there," he said. They did, and I didn't object.

That night, I thought a lot about the earlier years of our marriage. In 1976, Dick and I moved out into the country, 4 miles north of Creighton, Missouri. We built our own house there. In 1985, it was struck by lightning and burned to the ground. At first, we were devastated. Then Dick and I decided to do it all over again. We built a new house from the ground up, on 40 acres of farmland. The experience knit our family together. The ministry, I worried, might pull us apart.

The fact is, when I started to pastor, Dick got even more involved in the Creighton church than he had been previously.

It was as if he felt he had to cover the jobs I had been doing as well as his own. He became chair of both the staff-parish relations committee and the church board. But he also started helping at Calhoun, too. Dick showed up to move pews and swap out the carpet. He was there to serve some of the church dinners. But on Sunday mornings, Dick was at Creighton—except when our grandchildren were baptized, that is.

Cody quit looking for a replacement and, at the annual conference, I was assigned to both churches for the next year. It was a quarter-time assignment—10 hours a week, with five hours designated for each church. Over the months of that first year or two, the churches' members stopped worrying that I would leave them.

Chapter 6

CODY AND I, along with Pastor Jeff Brinkman from Woods Chapel in Lee's Summit, were driving to the conference offices in Columbia when the district superintendent asked how things were going.

"All right," I responded, "except Calhoun really needs a roof."

Jeff interjected that a guy in his congregation, Roland Hess, had just approached him about feeling like he needed to give more. Jeff called Roland and, the next thing I knew, Roland was perched on Calhoun's steep, shingled roof.

"How much money do you have?" Roland yelled.

"Ten thousand dollars," I replied, knowing that it wouldn't come close to covering the roofing expenses.

"That will do," he countered, "and what it won't cover, I will."

I'll never forget the day I was able to tell the congregation that the roof was going to be taken care of with the funds we had. It was like removing a haze—like taking off your sunglasses and seeing how bright everything is in the sunlight.

The attitude improved. People stopped talking about what they couldn't do.

A work group of mostly Hispanic men showed up a couple of weeks later. They stayed three nights in the hotel in Clinton and worked four full days replacing our roof. Several women of the church cooked meals for the hard-working crew each day.

After the roof project, we were flabbergasted to learn that someone had named Calhoun as a beneficiary in his will. No one ever imaged that this man had two nickels to rub together—and then we learned that "Zeek" left the church $70,000!

Since the money was an unexpected gift, we decided to use some of it to help out a few people in the neighborhood. Then the church began its own extreme makeover. Down came the dirty drapes and the grey insulation. The rotted windows were removed too, and energy-efficient ones replaced them. The badly worn red carpeting was yanked up and the original hardwood floors were restored. The tin ceiling was also touched up. Both the interior and the exterior of the building were freshly painted. Two tiny bathrooms—downstairs, in the fellowship hall—were converted into one large restroom, accessible to those with disabilities. A closet upstairs was converted into a bathroom. Much to my delight, the church was equipped with hot water for the first time ever.

Momentum began to take over. Churchgoers were so excited to show off their place of worship that a section of the sanctuary was redesigned as a welcome area. People came early. They smiled more. They went to lunch with one another after service. Other people in the neighborhood grew curious about all of the activity, and some of them started to come in.

Calhoun members put $20,000 into a certificate of deposit in case there was an emergency. They had been very good stewards. Light began streaming in and out of the once-dark church.

CONTENTS

COME UNTO ME

Chapter 7

WITH ALL OF the physical changes happening at Calhoun, there was an awakening of the people. They were seeing things as if for the first time, and they began to dream about how things could be.

"What if we put stained glass windows inside the new, clear-paned ones that were just installed?" a member asked, right out loud. A gifted artist was contacted, and a set of panels was designed that nicely matched the stained glass window on the front of the church. Soon thereafter, members of the congregation starting "adopting" individual windows in memory of their parents or in honor of their children and grandchildren. One by one, the warm colors from each newly installed design began to bathe the sanctuary.

Bishop Robert Schnase preached at Calhoun on the morning that the church dedicated its renovated space. A celebrated author, the bishop preached a powerful sermon and he baptized six people during the service. What a day of rejoicing it was! Actually, every service that includes a baptism is a time of celebration, and during that time, our district superintendent was performing most of the baptisms. There have been couples, babies, young children and even teenagers baptized by our district superintendent, the Rev. Cody Collier. After a 17-year-old girl was baptized one week, she was joined by her mother and grandmother the next. A 30-year-old, single man also had decided to be baptized. Every occasion is different, but the reaction of the church is always the same: There is pure joy.

One morning, a man approached me before worship and asked if I would come by his house. He needed to talk to me, he said. I was in the mix of moving, but I told him that I would stop by. Unfortunately, I didn't make it that week. On Sunday, I was a little sheepish as he addressed me once more. "It's OK," he said. "I know you are really busy right now."

"I'll be there tonight," I promised.

Well, the afternoon got away from me, and so did the evening. I called and told him that I would be there the next day, and we set a time. Not knowing anything about the subject for the meeting and having failed to show up both times I was expected, I grew a little anxious that night. When I arrived, I waited outside in the car for a few minutes beforehand, asking for God's guidance.

We had a cordial visit for about a half an hour, and then the reason he asked me to come over surfaced. "Margie, can you baptize an almost-80-year-old man?"

Lay ministers are not permitted to baptize. They must have someone who is ordained present to do so. "*I* can't," I said, "but I know plenty of people who can!"

He wanted to keep the baptism low-key. I wasn't to tell anyone in the congregation. The only thing that anyone present would have picked up on that morning was that a retired pastor and his wife were visiting us for worship. When the proper time came, I asked the pastor to come forward, and then we shared the joyous news of the baptism with the entire church.

There were gasps of approval as he committed his life to Christ in a strong and loud voice.

In the 10 years since 2006, the Calhoun Church has celebrated 60 baptisms, 16 re-affirmations of faith and 30 letters of transfer. Drake's Chapel has had eight baptisms and 15 transfers during that same time.

"To God be the glory."

Chapter 8

DRAKE'S CHAPEL WAS feeling a little left out. Because their church had a healthy endowment fund, the church building was well maintained inside and out. Consequently, they weren't experiencing the excitement of renovations or new Sunday visitors. I told them that they already had something that should attract people, but that they hadn't leveraged it: their pastoral setting.

"Why don't we have an ice cream social?" I asked. "Once people experience the tranquility of this place, they will be hooked."

We purchased an advertisement for the event in the *Clinton Daily Democrat*, a newspaper that covers local news. "Join us for singing and ice cream under the stars," our advertisement stated, and the other pertinent information followed.

That Sunday evening, roughly 50 children and adults sat on folding chairs in the church parking lot, surrounded by tall trees. There were no bulletins or hymnals. We didn't use a lectern or a pulpit. People just called out the names of their favorite hymns, and we sang their first verses for about an hour. When it was time for a treat, people pulled out freezers full of peach, chocolate, vanilla and burnt sugar ice cream. They produced all kinds of toppings for the worshippers, too: hot fudge, butterscotch, whipped cream, cherries and bananas. It was hard to tell if the people liked the dessert more or the chance to build fellowship. They lingered a long time.

Marsha and Bill were among those assembled that night. They had moved to Missouri from Kansas two years before, and although they had attended a church in Clinton a couple of times, they hadn't found a church home. Something must have moved them that evening, because they became regulars at Drake's Chapel. A few months later, they approached me about joining the church. In talking with them, Bill shared that his mother didn't think he had been baptized. She had located all of the certificates for her other children, but couldn't find any baptismal records for him.

I invited my former pastor Barbara Bowser, an ordained elder, to assist me on the Sunday Marsha and Bill were set to join the church. Bill, ever the prankster, had a huge surprise for me. He arrived at the church wearing flippers on his feet and goggles covering his eyes, as if I was going to dunk him in the ocean. His antics brought laughter and joy into the congregation.

Later that year, we learned that Bill's cancer, which had been in remission, had returned. It meant that he would have to undergo months of chemotherapy and radiation. To make matters worse, Bill didn't have coverage to pay for his medications. Fortunately, Drake's Chapel had started a special fund that reserved 1 percent of the church's income for assisting people during a crisis. We then established a Make-a-Difference committee to confidentially review requests and distribute money from the fund. The committee members decided to pay for Bill's prescriptions from the local pharmacy.

Soon, Marsha and Bill were unable to attend worship. Bill was just too ill, and incredibly weak. The cancer had metastasized. That's when we found the "big" of being small. If there was no way for Marsha and Bill to attend worship, then we would take church to their farm. They had acres of beautifully wooded land that backed up to Sandy Creek.

After worshipping at Calhoun, we skipped the regular service at Drake's Chapel. Some of the Calhoun crowd joined me as I drove directly to Marsha and Bill's place. Others came who weren't a part of Drake's Chapel, either—they were just neighbors and friends who wanted to participate.

No one who was there that morning will forget our church in the timber. A simple cross sat on a table that had been moved out of Bill and Marsha's home. The sound of the birds and the wind rustling the trees was our music. I had purchased a new communion chalice and plate for the occasion while I was at Lake Junaluska for a Board of Church and Society meeting. The glassware was handmade and the glaze made them shine.

Unfortunately, I shipped the communion set home and when it arrived, the chalice was shattered to pieces. I was heartbroken. I had imagined that they would be perfect for the outdoor service. It dawned on me later that God had had a better idea. I used the broken container. In fact, I busted it more. Before people stepped forward to receive the elements, I told the story of the smashed chalice and how I realized that Holy Communion was about being broken. "Each person who comes to receive today," I said, "is also broken. This holy meal is the only way we become whole once more."

After the 50-some people had received the bread and juice, a basket was passed so that each person could take a piece of the ruined chalice home, to remember the time we had spent in the timbers and with Bill.

Chapter 9

IN A SMALL community, a pastor claims everyone. Over the years, the Windsor Funeral Home had asked me to officiate at more and more services for the unchurched. The children at the Bullseye convenience store began to recognize me when I stopped in for an iced tea. Clerks and schoolteachers knew my name. I felt like a celebrity.

The same held true at the local hospital. One day, when I was at Golden Valley Memorial Hospital in Clinton, visiting a church family in the emergency room, I remembered that someone had shared that Aileen Lacks from the City of Calhoun had also been admitted. The Lackses were delightful people, and devoted Roman Catholics. Charles was a retired physician. The whole town referred to him as "Doc." Each year, our congregation would stop by their home to sing Christmas carols.

I told my emergency room family that I would be back, and headed up to check in on Aileen. As I got onto the elevator, I saw Doc. He, too, was going to see his wife. A nurse saw the two of us walking down the hallway together and shook her head so that I would know that Aileen had passed. We continued to walk. When we entered her room, I took Doc's hand and told him that Aileen was dead.

"She's gone?" he asked.

I nodded and said, "Aileen couldn't wait. She is gone."

He approached the bed, bent down, and gave her the sweetest kiss. Then he turned to me, with tears rolling down his cheeks. "I was married 72 years to the best woman on earth."

I asked him if I could pray with him. "Yes, please," was his response.

The Holy Spirit interceded for me. I really don't remember what I said. We talked for another 30-40 minutes after that, while we waited for his family to arrive. It was sacred time. After I left Doc, I phoned their Catholic church to make sure that the priest had been notified about Aileen. The parish had just received a new priest, and I wanted to make sure he had the chance to be seen as their spiritual leader. Small towns tend to make ministers and their people ecumenical.

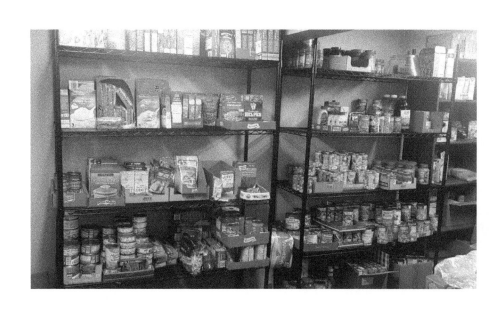

Chapter 10

WHEN MOST PEOPLE think about poverty, they envision poor people in the city: homeless men sleeping on a park bench or under a freeway viaduct; senior citizens cramped in small apartments, deciding whether to spend their money on medicine or food or heat; single mothers and little children who lack decent shoes and are forced to rely on public transportation. Maybe these images aren't accurate for the urban poor, but rural poverty faces a very different, and possibly worse, problem: Almost no one even thinks about rural poverty.

Rural poverty exists in small towns and on family farms. The poor work at gas stations and at convenience stores. They hold government jobs. In our region of Missouri, Clinton is the county seat. Some are employed at the hospital, and others work at the cheese factory, 9 miles away. The poor have jobs, but their wages are low and their hours are often limited. This isn't generally true for farmers, but farmhands are frequently paid poorly. Eighty percent of the families in the churches' areas live below the poverty line. One hundred percent of the children in Calhoun receive free or discounted lunches at school.

"Can we start a food pantry?" one of the leaders asked one day, in the middle of a church board meeting.

People had noticed the success of the Harvesters food distribution program, on the second Friday of each month, and many were eager to begin our food pantry. Farmers and churches helped by donating bags of bread and vegetables that were near their expiration dates. Congregation members also observed that their neighbors needed staples, and that many people were in trouble at the end of the month when their income was spent and their refrigerator was empty.

We began collecting food from both Drake's Chapel and Calhoun on the third Sunday of each month, for a fourth-Friday distribution. At first, we stored the cans of chicken, tuna, spaghetti sauces with meat and anything else that contained protein in a closet in the basement. It became apparent almost instantly, though, that the program needed a bigger area, and so the pantry took over one of the classrooms.

Celura and Leroy Books became the driving force behind the pantry. They augmented the congregations' donations with bread, hamburger and other meats that were on sale. Soon, our pantry had stocked boxes of Kleenex, bags of toilet paper, paper towels and personal hygiene items, too—items not covered with food stamps. The Books, along with other dedicated volunteers, stuffed bags full of food and household products—each appropriate for the size of a family. Then, they opened the church doors at 5 p.m. and invited people to come in. Working people stopped by on their way home. Those helping recorded the names and number of family members of the recipients, but we never required them to complete long forms or provide identification. They were our neighbors.

Chapter 11

WE WERE EXCITED to offer a one-day Vacation Bible School (VBS), after many years had passed without the summertime Christian education program. To announce its debut, posters were designed, printed and hung all over town. Verna, a regular Sunday school teacher and an occasional soloist during worship, had organized simple songs with hand motions for the students. Debbie had collected all of the materials for a craft project. Bottles of glue, skeins of yarn, colored construction paper and an assortment of picture frames were arranged on the tables, so that the students could make religious art to hang on their refrigerator doors.

Billie had even borrowed a couple of books from the library to plan her session. She was in charge of recreation. Without a gym, she had prepared outdoor activities. Martha, Iris and Sherrelyn had planned a nutritionally balanced lunch and an afternoon snack, complete with red Kool-Aid. Of course, you can't run a VBS without a Bible story or two, and sharing Scripture readings was going to be my job.

Ready. Set. Stop.

That Saturday morning, just one student showed up. But Debbie was not to be defeated.

She jumped into her car and drove around town, literally summoning every child she saw on the gravel roads until she returned to the church with six more children. I wish I had a video of the reaction of the volunteers. They jumped and cheered as if we had just won a huge sports championship. There were only seven students, and many churches would have considered the day a failure. We didn't. It was a great day for the children and the adults.

They sat in a semicircle on the sanctuary hard wood floor. Their legs were folded under them pretzel-style. The children listened to the Bible reading and I showed them the illustrations as I completed each page. Their attention span wasn't long though and, fortunately, the story wasn't either. Arts and crafts was a definite hit with the girls. The boys were happy to get outside with Billie to compete. Lunch was loud for only seven students, but it was definitely nice to hear the children talking and laughing. It was wonderful to hear them singing, too. Some of the songs Verna selected were ones I learned in Granna's church.

On Sunday, during the Joys and Concerns period, several of the adult volunteers talked about their experiences with our Vacation Bible School. One woman quoted a little boy who had attended and announced that it had been the best day of his life. The following year, 24 children attended VBS.

Chapter 12

WORSHIP BEGAN TO change. On any given Sunday, you could find men in nice Dockers and sport shirts—or in bibs, jeans or shorts. There were people in the pews who were pierced and tattooed; others kept their hair long or had beards. A few had no hair at all. Women came in dresses and skirts, but also in pants and shorts—and, in October, some people even wore Halloween costumes.

There was a man attending Calhoun who wasn't a member, but surely was one of us. I knew the minute he walked in the door that he was the answer to my 7-year prayer: I had begged God to send us a guitar player. This man had only played in bars before, coming into the church looking as if he could have walked on stage with ZZ Top. But a couple of Sundays a month, he offered a fresh song right out of his heart. On many Sundays, he sang a song that he had written after being inspired by the Scripture reading for the week. There were tears all around on the morning he sang, "When God's People Pray."

Worship also started to feel fun. I began using a yellow bag every Sunday morning during the children's time. I put all kinds of things inside one of three different sized yellow bags, and the kids would try and guess what the contents were. One Sunday I had an object that was entirely flat in the smallest bag. When I asked for guesses, young Clayton replied, "I think it's a chicken."

I dare say that the entire congregation got their tickle box turned over, and it took a very long time to get them right side up again. At this point, I don't even remember what was in the bag. It didn't matter anyway.

One year, we had the Easter sunrise service on the rolling hills at Drake's Chapel. It was a beautiful setting, even if it was just a little bit chilly. My grandson Avery was in attendance that morning. A member of the church had given him an Easter basket, and when Avery got a little restless—as 18-month-olds do—the basket provider opened the bottle of bubbles that had been lodged in the basket's grass. In no time flat, Avery had bubbles floating in every direction, as we celebrated the risen savior.

At Calhoun, one special woman named Martha was both a painter and a knitter. We have two of her paintings in the church, and I have another one of them in my home. I can't count how many pairs of house shoes she knitted, so that I could give them to people in the hospital. She even took it upon herself to knit a pair for every woman in the congregation. For her birthday, the women honored her one Sunday by wearing their slippers to worship. She glowed with pride all morning.

Another Sunday I decided to mix it up a bit, and I disappeared during the service. When I came back into the sanctuary for the Scripture time, I was dressed like the woman at the well. I told the story in the first-person narrative, with a few additions from the "gospel according to Margie." One longtime member commented that it didn't even sound like me. I did something similar with the Good Samaritan text. I laid down on the elevated floor near the altar and delivered the whole message on my back, as if I was the crime victim left for dead in the ditch.

It became customary for me to call people up to the front for prayer if they were going through a rough time. If someone was about to be admitted into the hospital for surgery, for instance, the church would lay hands on him or her as we encircled that person. Even though I go to the hospital to pray with patients and their families, it is something entirely different to be surrounded by members of the church, as they intercede for you.

It has become a tradition during the Christmas Eve service for family groups to receive Holy Communion together. Members always watch for singles and graft them into their families. After communion is finished, I offer an individual prayer and a blessing for each family. The service isn't long. It does take a little extra time to include the family prayers, but the people have grown to love and expect them.

Chapter 13

I WAS WORN out as I made my way down the aisle of a filled-to-capacity flight after the 2008 South Central Jurisdictional Conference of the United Methodist Church. I wedged myself into the dreaded middle seat. As I juggled my things around, the man in the window seat looked up. It was Adam Hamilton. Suddenly, I experienced a burst of adrenaline and I realized that I had the best seat on the plane. Little did I know how the seating arrangement would change my churches.

I had known Adam from the very beginning of his ministry, in the Missouri West Annual Conference. Our small church in Creighton had been a partner in the launch of his new church, the Church of the Resurrection. In fact, I had been present that first Sunday for worship, in a funeral home on State Line Road. Since then, Adam's expanded, multi-site congregation had grown to become the largest United Methodist church in the country—and he had become a Methodist standout. His books, study guides and videos were Cokesbury bestsellers. He had become a popular preacher and a sought-after speaker.

Adam asked me what I had been doing. I started to talk with him about Calhoun and Drake's Chapel when he flipped open his laptop and said, "What did you say your cell phone number was?"

I was temporarily confused, because I didn't remember giving it, but offered the number to him anyway. I had no idea why he wanted it.

"May I call you next week and set up an appointment for my video team to come out and film you and your churches?" he asked, with sparkling eyes.

My mind was racing. Why would Adam Hamilton want to record my two small, rural churches? He explained to me that when he went to speak at different conferences around the country, people were always saying that their churches weren't like the Church of the Resurrection. They were small-membership churches. They couldn't relate to the size or scope of his ministries. He wanted to give them some examples of vibrant ministries on a smaller scale.

After we arrived in Kansas City, I hopped on a commuter bus to retrieve my car from the parking lot, but my thoughts stayed on the conversation with Adam.

Adam called the next week, as he had promised. He told me that nothing needed to be done on our end. His film crew would video some of both worship services and talk with a few of the people before worship at Drake's Chapel and after worship at Calhoun. The congregation members began to clean every crack and crevice in anticipation of their creative company.

The crew was amazing. They made interviewees comfortable and relaxed. I was nervous, so much so that I thought once, at Drake's Chapel, that I was going to throw up. I remember trying to decide whether I should try and make it downstairs to the bathroom or go outside and risk someone seeing me. Even though I knew that the crew would not be filming the sermon, it would be the first time that cameras were rolling while I was speaking, and it made me anxious.

On the way to Calhoun, the camera team followed me. I prayed the whole time, "Please, God, don't let me mess this up and ruin the story of what these churches have done." As I got out of my car, a bulletin was caught by the wind. It blew up in the air and cut my face just above the lip. *Oh, great,* I thought. *What next?*

Things went smoothly at Calhoun. Parishioners were natural as they spoke about their love of the church and of what God was doing. It was my turn when all the others were finished. I felt like I was in a courtroom, trying to answer just the questions they posed. As the crew packed up their cameras and microphones, I asked them how Adam would use the footage. They responded that Adam would let us know when it was ready.

A letter arrived in the mail. It was an invitation to attend the Leadership Institute at the Church of the Resurrection. Five tickets were included—one for me, and two for each church. We were so excited. During the presentation, Adam started talking about me and the two churches. Then the video burst onto a huge screen behind him. I was terrified. I remembered the wind, the cut, the knot in my stomach—and the urge to vomit suddenly surfaced again. At the end of the three-minute video, there was thunderous applause. Adam asked my parishioners and me to stand up and be recognized. All the things I had been worried about were suddenly gone. It was never about me in the first place.

That Saturday night was only the beginning, though. Adam shared the video everywhere he went. I began receiving text messages and Facebook messages from people all over the country. They had viewed the footage at an Annual Conference or some training session, and they contacted me to congratulate us or to ask for consultation on what to try in their local setting. It validated our ministry. It challenged us, too. One Sunday at church, I talked about a stranger in another state calling me, after having seen the video. One of my parishioners later commented, "We have to really watch the way we walk now, because others are watching us."

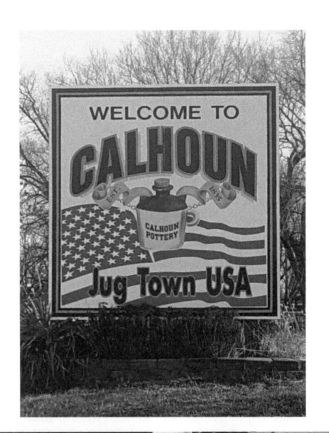

WELCOME TO
CALHOUN
CALHOUN POTTERY
Jug Town USA

DRAKES CHAPEL
UNITED METHODIST CHURCH

Chapter 14

IN A SMALL town, there are traditions and events that go back for generations. For instance, at one time Calhoun was nicknamed "Jugtown." Its clay was almost perfect for making pottery, and large amounts of earthenware were shipped all over the country from one of six area companies. When these businesses closed, there was a festival held for many years afterward that drew people from near and far. They wanted to see the famous jugs—and some wanted to purchase them. I am in possession of a few pieces, but none of them are originals.

I grew up just 7 miles away from Calhoun, in another small town called Windsor. Although I don't recall my family going to the pottery festivals, I couldn't wait to attend the annual Calhoun Colt Show. I mostly remember that there was a merry-go-round and that, once I was older, I got the chance to ride the Ferris wheel. There was always a parade with bands and floats, politicians and a queen.

According to its organizers, the festival in Calhoun is the "oldest of its kind in Missouri." I've been told that more than 100 years ago, two farmers were arguing about who had the better colt, and they decided to settle the matter by meeting up in the town square. The townspeople would determine who had bragging rights. And the rest, as they say, is history.

My churches have been involved in the three-day celebration every year. Calhoun has housed the all-school reunions that meet on the Saturday night, and most years, its parishioners have built a float for the Grand Parade, too. One year in particular, both Calhoun and Drake's Chapel entered floats. The parade route isn't very long, and so I traveled with the Calhoun float to the finish. Then, I took off my top-layer Calhoun T-shirt and ran to the tail end of the parade, sporting the Drake's T-shirt that had been underneath. I'm not sure if it was the layers or the four-block sprint, but by the time I climbed onto the Drake's float my face was redder than the T-shirt I was wearing.

Local people know that there is a children's parade that occurs before the grand parade, when the kids show up with their pets, decorated bikes and, cutest of all, their adorned doll buggies. A bystander told me last year that she remembered when there were 20 doll buggies all decked out and vying for the grand prize. That year there were only two, and one wasn't a buggy at all—rather, it was a stroller that the child was pushing.

After the parades, we are always busy with our homemade tenderloin sandwich lunch, but the activities continued with folks from all over bringing their mules, colts and goats to compete for the blue ribbon—the Colt Show's most coveted prize. There are still more activities down at the city's arena, like the horseshoe contest that takes up the entire weekend.

There is also a baby contest. We all know that there has only been one most beautiful, charming, cute-as-a-button baby, and every mother has it. For the contest, infant and toddler boys and girls are separated and put into appropriate age groups. The little girls are dressed to the nines, and the little boys don suspenders and knickers—and some wear tuxedo shirts. Each age group ends up with first-, second- and third-place winners.

Every year on the Sunday of the festival, there is a community church service on the grounds of the old courthouse. The first year I was at Calhoun, it was my turn to preach. I so remember that there were several folks present that year, and some years since, who were not too happy about a woman delivering the sermon.

In later years, I have tried my luck at winning a blue ribbon in the Colt Show's culinary events. I have entered bread, cookies and other items. The best I have done so far is second place. In 2016, the Calhoun church sponsored a funnel cake stand on the square to raise money to help Quinn, a 4-year old girl in the preschool who was undergoing treatment for a brain tumor. The cake sales raised $300. The offering from the community church service was also designated for Quinn and her family. Later in the year, the Calhoun congregation raised over $1,000 for her at the church's fall festival.

Chapter 15

IN 2010, I came to believe that we should try and do something for the children in the community for Christmas. There are only two churches in Calhoun, and many of the children in the town and surrounding area didn't attend either. So I talked with the church leadership about throwing a birthday party for Jesus, and they agreed to give it a try. Over time, permission-giving had become their custom.

We started small. We invited the children to come with their parents and hear the biblical story of Christmas at the church. I read the story from Luke, and the children surrounded me. Then we escorted them downstairs to the Fellowship Hall, where each child was allowed to pick out gifts, purchased by the parishioners, to give to their parents and siblings. The event finished off with a hot dog lunch, a birthday cake and singing "Happy Birthday" to Jesus.

As the years passed, more and more youngsters came to the party. Then, one year, a grandmother who was waiting to pick up her grandchild mentioned that it would be nice if there was something similar for grandparents on a fixed income, so that they could give gifts to their little ones. Why didn't we think of that?

For several years now, entire families have had the chance to shop. Have some been a little greedy in the new process? Oh, yes, a few. But we have developed checkpoints to minimize abuse. The room is arranged so that the more expensive gifts are displayed on one table and the other presents are put out in other areas. This way, each shopper can take one special gift for their parent, child, sibling or grandchild, and still have the opportunity to take several other, less expensive, gifts as well.

Gifts now are donated by members of both congregations as well as their relatives and friends, along with community members. Donors buy presents all year long and take advantage of sales and specials. For Christmas in 2016, nearly 700 gifts were wrapped and sent home with area residents to tuck under their Christmas trees, ready for eager hands to open. Probably the best part for me, though, is listening to the happy chorus of, "Happy birthday, dear Jesus. Happy birthday to you!"

Once the Christmas party was successful and routine, I asked the leadership to try an outreach event for Easter. Again, we invited the neighborhood children. We actually had them register for this event, so that we could collect their information—name, address, age, etc.—and break up the group by ages in advance. We didn't want the smallest children trampled by the bigger kids!

As with the Christmas party, I read the Bible story while the other adults were busy—this time, with hiding eggs and chocolates. Then the hunt began, with running and screaming. The children returned with jam-packed baskets to Fellowship Hall, where they broke open their plastic eggs and nibbled on pieces of candy. I couldn't help but compare the time it took for older, arthritic hands to fill the eggs and the instant it took for young, excited fingers to break them open. The candy-eating was interrupted as the children with Kool-Aid mustaches were ushered into a separate room filled with bats, balls, books and just about every little gift that one could imagine. Claiming several prizes from the second area, one boy exclaimed, "This is wonderful! I'm so glad Jesus isn't dead."

Have all of these children joined our church? No, but they have heard the stories of Jesus and they have experienced the love of our congregations. Seeds have been planted.

Chapter 16

RURAL COMMUNITIES DON'T have much diversity. I prayed and prayed about that. How could I introduce the people of my churches to others who were different than they were? Then one day, at a General Board of Church and Society meeting in Washington, D.C., the Rev. Faith Fowler asked if she could bring a youth group to our church to do a mission project. Faith pastors a church in Detroit, and she was concerned that her teens rarely leave the city and that they had never had the chance to experience a small town. She also said that mission teams were always coming to her community and so it was important for her people to have the chance to experience mission from the "giving" side. Faith is not only the pastor of a downtown congregation, Cass Community United Methodist Church; she is also the executive director of Cass Community Social Services, a nonprofit that provides food, housing, jobs, health and mental health care to thousands of people each month.

In anticipation of our visitors' arrival, we borrowed cots from the local armory and converted the Sunday school rooms into sleeping quarters. We made arrangements with the high school so the team members could use the gym showers, and we sought out jobs for the team to accomplish. The youth group was slated to clean gutters for area seniors and pick up garbage on empty lots, but mostly they would work with Hank, an elderly man who lived down the street from the Calhoun building. Hank lived in a mobile home with dangerous steps. The youth from Cass would have to take down the rotten stairs and construct a new set so he could get in and out of his home safely.

The 13-member youth group arrived late one summer night in a small, white bus that was covered in a coat of dust from the dirt roads. The bus was crowded full of people, their luggage and plenty of tools—hammers, nails, saws, measuring tapes and drills. The youth and their chaperones took over the church building for almost a week. They slept in our classrooms; changed in the bathrooms; cooked and ate in the basement; worshipped in the sanctuary. They especially liked the huge papier-mâché whale that occupied the front of the church near the altar and was left over from the Vacation Bible School program. What they didn't like was that none of their cell phones worked inside. In order to get reception, they had to go outside and stand in the middle of the street—one disadvantage of a town with just 400 residents.

Their days were spent doing manual labor, with the exception of several trips to the Amish lumberyard. The first trip there was a decision made by our Detroit friends to support local employment. The other trips were a result of their new interest in everything Amish—Amish dress, religion and community. I am sure the Amish employees were equally as curious about the group of mostly African-American members, which returned to the store each day. One of the young people from Detroit was amazed that the people from

Calhoun knew that they were outsiders without even talking to them.

In the evenings, we exposed the teenagers to people and places that we thought they would enjoy. One night, they visited a beekeeper who let them scrape the honey off of a comb and taste it fresh. One afternoon, when the team finished early, we took them to the lake and then for a hike on Katy Trail. Another evening, they were invited to a big barbecue cookout on the farm of one of our church members. There they learned about how to make hay and why it is so important in a farm community. While waiting for the meal to be ready, the young people played pool with Samantha, a teenager from the Calhoun congregation—and before anyone knew it, the kids were talking about visiting Detroit the following summer.

Since the entire Calhoun congregation had gotten to know the youth from Cass, it wasn't a hard sell to their parents or the church board. The teenagers sponsored a couple of fundraisers and I recruited adult chaperones and, before you knew it, we stuffed ourselves and our luggage into cars. We were Detroit bound!

Just as the stars in the dark countryside had dumbfounded the teenagers from Detroit, members of our youth group were surprised by the density and diversity of the city. They were taken back at first by the bars on windows and alarms on everything but they also noticed the architectural beauty of many of the buildings. They commented more than once that the people of Detroit were friendly.

We volunteered at Cass Community Social Services during the days. Our youth rode stationary bikes to generate electricity for the warehouse. They assisted the women and men of Green Industries in recycling tires and paper. We spent a day in the commercial kitchen assembling thousands of sandwiches and hot meals. One of our adult chaperones was a 74-year-old woman who had always wanted to be on a mission team. She worked as hard as everyone else.

We did the touristy things, too. The group visited the Heidelberg Project, an outside work of art that brings color and creativity to an otherwise deserted east side neighborhood. We went to Belle Isle to enjoy the Detroit River and catch a glimpse of Canada. One day, our kids took in a Tigers' game at Comerica Park.

The contrast of urban opportunities and architectural beauty with concentrated poverty was not lost on us. The trip was an eye-opening experience. The Calhoun kids learned every bit as much as the Detroit youth had, and they made new friends, too—even if they were cutthroat when playing Spoons.

Chapter 17

ONE SUNDAY MORNING, Calhoun's songbird, Georgia, was not her bubbly self. The concern she shared that Sunday stunned the congregation. She had cancer and it had spread all over her body. The word *terminal* hung over the sanctuary like a pall covering a casket. We couldn't believe it. We had to do something. What could we do? How could we help?

Georgia's family lived in Colorado. We purchased a plane ticket so that she could go stay at her son's home. Billie, Pearl and I took her to the airport with just a few pieces of clothing in her bag. She was her usual sweet self, but extremely weak. Billie managed to get clearance to take her to the gate, and they even let her help Georgia get situated in her seat before leaving her. Pearl and I waited until the two were out of sight before tears started streaming.

Once she was gone, the parishioners re-directed their attention to Georgia's things. She had assisted church members in separating the belongings she wanted to keep from what she wanted to sell. The women of Drake's Chapel and Calhoun organized a whale of a rummage sale. They arranged clothing, put prices on kitchen appliances, polished furniture and more. With a little advertising, shoppers came out in droves. When the sale concluded, the event had raised nearly $3,000 for Georgia.

Men from both churches loaded the items she wanted to retain onto a U-Haul truck. They also hitched a trailer to the back of the truck so Georgia's car could be towed to Colorado at the same time. With no experience driving a truck or pulling a car, I volunteered to take the wheel, with Billie as copilot. Iris and Scott would follow behind in a van, which would also bring us back to Missouri.

After the truck was unloaded at our destination, we gathered together with Georgia's son, Steve, and many of the men who helped unpack the truck. We offered up prayers of thanksgiving for the traveling mercies and for the love of Christ. We shared communion, too. It was a special and sacred time. Yet I was glad to return the rental truck keys after we were done and to be just a passenger on the way back home.

Two weeks later, I received a call while a group of us were filling Christmas baskets. It was Steve. Our sweet Georgia's victory was won. A group of us went back to Colorado to help celebrate her wonderful life. It was a bit strange for me, because I had been asked to speak and no woman had ever brought the message in her son's church. He explained that he had been so impressed by the tasks my churches had taken on to help his mother that he wanted me to deliver the eulogy.

"I know you think we were good to your mother. I want you to understand that people loved her in our church," I started, "and she loved God. Georgia trusted God for everything. She would pray and wait for an answer. Unlike most of us, if she didn't hear anything from God, she didn't proceed. Georgia had a patient faith. I think that's why she had such an interesting life. I know that she has gone on to eternal life and that we now are the ones who must trust God."

Chapter 18

IT IS PRETTY easy to get in a rut in ministry. Ministers need to be disciplined about praying for the congregation and community. There are always jobs around the church building and correspondence needing replies. Bulletins must be prepared, printed, folded and made ready for Sunday mornings. Time is required to read and re-read the Scripture passages, in order to write a sermon. I try to start writing the message at least by Wednesday of each week. The first week of the month—at least, in most churches—also means Holy Communion, and so there are extra preparations.

A dear saint at the Creighton United Methodist Church Alma Sloan always made the Communion bread. It made Communion special for me and for the members of the church. She continued this ministry well into her 90s, even after she had lost her sight. I believe she found making the loaf as meaningful as we did. Unfortunately for us, Alma eventually moved into an assisted-living facility in Kansas to be closer to her daughter.

I climbed out of a rut when I took over the task of making Communion bread. I used my grandmother's method. When I was a child, Granna would make fresh, homemade bread daily. The soothing aroma of baking bread would fill the house. In making the dough, she taught me to push out those things that would keep me from the love of God and to fold into my life the things that the Lord would find pleasing.

Today, I make the bread for both of my churches. As I make the bread, I pray for each person who will partake of the holy meal and for the visitors who will be in attendance, hungry and longing for things unknown to me but known by our Creator. It has very much become a spiritual discipline for me.

Recently, one of the members of Drake's Chapel asked if I would visit a senior citizen named Jo and her daughter Grace. He had done some work for them and had mentioned how I had been with him at the hospital when he had had cancer surgery. He said that I had anointed and prayed with him, and that it had given him great comfort.

The 93-year-old mother, Jo, asked him if he thought I would anoint and pray for her. He indicated that he was sure I would stop by. When the parishioner and I arrived at the home of Jo and Grace, both women were overjoyed. It was a precious time for all of us in their home, which seemed to have "the sweet scent of Jesus" as we say here. There was just a Christian aura in the living room. A well-worn Bible sat open on the table next to Jo's favorite chair.

Their home was also special for all of the pictures that hung on the walls and that were displayed on the furniture. There were photos from Jo's childhood. Josephine was one of three children, and I learned that one of her sisters used to sit by my granna in the Windsor church. Jo got married, I gathered from another print, when she was 22. Her husband's name was Stoestle, but no one could pronounce it, and that's why everyone referred to him as "SP." He died in 2005, but they had been blessed with eight children.

Jo pointed out the framed picture she had of her parents. She told stories about them that made me understand how much she loved them, missed them and how the memory of them gave her strength.

"Folks were plain mean back then," she said, referring to some of the racism they had had to endure. I wondered whether her parents had been slaves in Missouri, but didn't feel that it was my place to ask. The Missouri Compromise had cost countless families their freedom as the nation expanded westward.

When I was leaving, I remember thinking that it was the first week of the month and that we would be serving Communion on Sunday. The local pastor from Clinton consecrated the elements for Calhoun and since I always take Communion to shut-ins and to nursing homes after church, I asked them if they would like me to bring them Communion. "I don't remember when I last had the Lord's Supper!" she exclaimed, with tears in her eyes. "Please come."

There were many places to take Communion that Sunday, and so I arrived at Jo's house late in the day. It didn't matter, though. We had a marvelous time together—quoting Scripture, singing, laughing, praying and, of course, sharing the holy meal. The prayers were powerful. The Spirit of the Lord seemed to be rattling the rafters in the home of those precious women.

Until I met Jo and Grace, I hadn't thought about people outside my two churches who might want Communion. It was a revelation for me. There is no way I would ever miss taking Communion to these two women again. It blesses me, and whoever accompanies me, as well as Jo and Grace.

Not long ago, when I was out of town, I received a call from Grace. One of Jo's daughters-in-law had passed away suddenly, and she wanted help telling her mom. I told her that I was away but that I would send Billie, one of our Congregational Care Ministers, to be there. Grace was appreciative that I could send someone—and so was I.

Chapter 19

IT IS SO easy to be consumed by what a small-membership church cannot do. There are just not enough people to do everything that needs to be done. This was especially true of Calhoun, because the building required so many repairs. Ever since someone had stepped forward to lend a hand with the roof replacement, though, the church members had begun looking for ways to encourage others.

When I was still at Creighton United Methodist Church, I suggested that both the Creighton United Methodist Women and the Lucas United Methodist Women sponsor a back-to-school luncheon for teachers. The first year, they served salads and desserts. The next year, they progressed to baked potatoes with all the fixings, salads and desserts, for the day before the students returned to school. Throughout the year, teachers, staff, administrators and board members could request prayer partners from the churches. The two women's groups continue to organize and carry out this event to this day.

After hearing about this outreach program, the women at Calhoun decided to try the same thing. In addition to the event for teachers and faculty, Calhoun added a student back-to-school event. At this event, a meal is supplied. Hygiene items are also given away—toothbrushes, toothpaste, combs and deodorant. The church has also supplied socks, and has barbers and hairstylists on hand to give free haircuts. Beyond this, if a student needed something during the school year, like a coat or boots or shoes, the counselor had my number and knew that we would handle it quickly and quietly.

Neither of my churches is wealthy, but when one local family had a sick child who needed to go to a hospital in Houston, Texas, Calhoun organized a fundraiser dinner and auction. When the meal was over, a total of $4,300 had been raised to get the child to the medical center for treatment.

A member at Calhoun once fell in the middle of the early morning hours. Her family member was unable to lift her, and called for help. An ambulance arrived promptly. The EMS team hoisted her up and got her back in bed in no time flat. Her heart was filled with gratitude. "They rescue people every night of the year," she said afterward. "Let's do something for them."

And so it was that the Calhoun church established a recognition night for first responders. All of the emergency personnel—EMTs, firefighters and police officers and their spouses were invited to a sit-down dinner. Each was presented a certificate of appreciation, along with a framed "Fireman's Prayer."

Chapter 20

IT WAS MEMORIAL Day, and I was visiting the Laurel Oaks Cemetery in Windsor with a friend when we were stopped by Dale and Sharon. Dale had been my brother's best friend during high school. I really didn't know him very well, except for the fact that he was always with my brother and that together, the two were cut-ups. I knew his wife, Sharon, much better.

We talked for a while, and then Dale asked me a question. "Do you do funerals for nonmembers?" he inquired.

My mind was scrambling. I knew that his family had belonged to a church of another denomination back in the 50s and 60s. Why would he be asking me this?

"Sure, I do lots of them," I answered. "Why do you ask?"

"Well, I want you to do mine, if you will. Can we talk about it sometime?"

It was not long after that that I found my way to Dale and Sharon's home. I had had no idea how sick he was. Hospice was already involved. Years of smoking had done a number on his lungs.

We had a long conversation about church subjects. Dale shared that he had held perfect attendance in Sunday school for 12 years, but that no one had ever asked if he wanted to be baptized. I simply couldn't believe it. We talked about the meaning of baptism. He confided that he didn't feel worthy of baptism, and I responded that no one is worthy of baptism— it's God's gift. I told him that I could ask someone to baptize him, and that the person could even come to the house, if he would like it. Dale responded that he wanted to think about it.

I continued to pray about Dale and baptism. When the first Sunday of the month came, I took Communion to our shut-ins—and something nudged me to visit Dale. His house was directly across the street from my last nursing-home stop. Actually, I wrestled with the idea for a few minutes. Would I be intruding? They hadn't contacted me. Maybe they would think I was being pushy.

Pulling into their driveway, I felt God's presence and knocked on the door, sure that it was the right thing to do.

"Well, hello there," Dale said, welcoming me. Little did I know at that time that those would be next to his last words on this side of heaven.

I spoke to Sharon for a while. She shared that Dale hadn't had a good night.

"Dale," I said, turning my attention to him. "Do you remember what we talked about the last time I was here?" There was no response from him, and so I repeated the question once more. I took hold of his hand and added, "Do you want to be baptized?"

There was a little jolt in his hand. What did that mean? Was he saying yes, or did it mean no? I looked at Sharon and told her that I interpreted the movement as an affirmation. I got the water and prepared to baptize him. I felt as unworthy as he had indicated he felt. I wasn't ordained, but during the final hours of a person's life, anyone is able to baptize.

Sharon stood on one side of the bed and I was on the other. I touched the baptismal water with my longest fingers and then moved them up to Dale's forehead. His skin was very warm, and I hoped the cool water would comfort him even as it cleansed him. I repeated the words I had heard all of my life: "I baptize you in the name of the Father, Son and Holy Spirit." The litany declared it. Baptism was an act of God.

Then I prayed. I prayed with all my heart and soul. I don't remember the exact words. but it was an emotional outpouring. "Amen," I concluded.

"Amen," said Sharon. I walked around Dale's bed to embrace her as she cried.

"Amen," Dale said, loud and clear, to our amazement.

It was a moment in time I will never forget. "Amen" was Dale's last word.

I received a call from Sharon only hours later, telling me that he had died. I don't know why no one ever asked him if he wanted to be baptized. I don't know why he left the Church. I don't know why he didn't try another congregation. Nor do I know why he sought me out, but I am sure that I made the right decision to stop that day. I had made the proper decision to baptize my brother's friend. Dale had wanted to be baptized.

Chapter 21

I HAVE NO idea when he first noticed it. The mole had been under his arm for years. He mentioned it to me in 2014, and I suggested that he get it checked out. Dick didn't like doctors, though. He really didn't like receiving help at all. His stint in the Army probably was to blame. In some ways, his time in the military scarred him permanently. He withdrew—never wanting to go out to eat or spend social time with friends. This wasn't true with the family, though. He was a great father and grandfather.

One afternoon, Dick came into the house with logs for the wood stove and remarked that the mole was bleeding. I didn't say anything. He could read my mind. He called our family doctor and went to the medical office, by himself. Without wasting time, the doctor removed the mole and sent it off for a biopsy. Dick returned to the office, alone, a week later. The diagnosis wasn't good. My husband had the worst kind of melanoma.

Surgery was required. They wanted to examine the lymph nodes around the mole area. I went with Dick for the outpatient procedure at the University of Kansas Medical Center (KUMC), right across the state line. We waited for a report for two weeks after the surgery. Finally, we learned that none of the nodes were infected.

Chemo was recommended nonetheless, as a precautionary step. Dick declined the treatments. I tried to persuade him to change his mind. I reminded him that he had worked for 30 years at General Motors, and that we deserved some time together. I told him that the children and grandchildren loved him and needed him. He could not be convinced.

For seven or eight months, he seemed healthy. Then he told me that he noticed blood when he used the bathroom. We returned to the doctor. Dick had a colonoscopy. Our physician reported that he had lost count of the number of tumors he observed.

After an MRI back at KU Medical Center, the results were shocking. Dick had a tumor at the top of his stomach and two on his brain. The doctor said that radiation was needed immediately. Dick agreed to taking a treatment. Even though the radiation zapped all of his energy, Dick then progressed to taking chemo in pill form. They made him deathly ill. He could barely walk. He fell more than once. He couldn't keep food down. Shingles appeared in his throat and he had to be hospitalized for a week. A second MRI indicated that the two tumors were shrinking, but that six new ones had appeared on his brain. Dick changed that day. The diagnosis destroyed him, and made him not himself; less than kind.

I kept working. Our son Richard's former wife, an RN, stepped in and provided tremendous support. One day in April, Dick—sick and in a rage—utterly destroyed the kitchen and living room. Dee said that we could take him to the emergency room or just call hospice. She contacted hospice, and they stepped right in. The staff members came in daily to check his vitals and help with bathing. A chaplain visited, too. As he was having difficulty resting, Dick was given stronger medication on the last Saturday of July. Only then did he begin sleeping through the night.

Billie called me at 8 a.m. one morning. She wanted to know how Dick was doing. I told her that he was still sleeping. She phoned once more at 9. She suggested I try to wake him. I couldn't, and I noticed a rattle in his breathing. I called hospice. The nurse was already on her way. When she arrived, without delay she ordered a suction machine for his lungs and a hospital bed for his body. After just two hours, the mechanical bed arrived. Several of Richard's friends were waiting to tenderly lift Dick out of his recliner and lay him down on the soft, clean sheets. He remained in the bed in the living room for the next week.

I called my newly appointed district superintendent, the Rev. Jim Simpson, and told him that I wouldn't be able to lead worship on Sunday morning. He preached in my place. What I didn't anticipate was how the church members would show up. Dick was semi-conscious, resting mostly, thanks to the new medication; but there was a constant coming and going of family members. Church members Iris and Pearl joined Billie and Dick's pastor, Betty, at the house. They did everything—answered the phone, prepared our food, cleaned the bathrooms, listened and loved us.

Despite the fact that I had ministered to families as they prepared for death, I had no idea that it was so close for Dick. He was more comfortable than he had been, even though his breathing was shallow. The nurse was monitoring his vital signs. I was talking to him, even though he was non-responsive at that point. I took his hand. Pearl touched his shoulder before going back into the kitchen.

I noticed that Dick's breathing was getting slower and slower as I looked over at Matt. He nodded, as if to tell me that he was watching. I really didn't know what I was talking about. We had all told Dick that it was OK to go and that we're all going to be all right. Suddenly, I felt Matt's hand on my shoulder. Almost in a whisper, he said, "He is in a better place now."

My son Richard and grandson Jacob were in the basement doing something. I asked someone to tell him to come up. Richard came bounding up the stairs and I told him that his dad was gone.

"What do you need?" Richard asked, and then temporarily lay down next to his father. After a couple of minutes, he composed himself and stood up. He summoned everyone in the house and asked them to surround Dick's bed, and announced, "We're not going to cry anymore. This is a victory." He finished by asking who wanted to pray.

I was paralyzed and, for once in my life, speechless. Billie prayed. Then she and an aide cleaned Dick up while we waited in the kitchen and out on the front porch. They washed his face, shaved him and combed his hair. We all said our good-byes before my Baptist friend from the Bradley & Hadley Funeral Home carried Dick's body out and placed it in the van. He had asked to be cremated.

Neither of my churches was large enough to accommodate the funeral meal. Dick's church couldn't handle it, either. The Rev. Brad Reed from the Clinton United Methodist Church offered to host the dinner in their Christian Life Center, and so that is where it was held. The Creighton congregation provided the meat. Drake's Chapel members brought salads and vegetables; Calhoun parishioners came with abundant desserts.

I had often wondered, as a pastor, if people felt like we were intruding on their private time when they were losing someone they love. What I discovered when it was my husband dying was that I was glad the un-anxious people were present, because they gave me strength when I wasn't sure I could go on. Every touch, every call, every card and every dish was invaluable to me and my family.

I liked to visit the Drake's Chapel sanctuary early in the morning or late in the afternoon. I'd move between the pews, sitting where parishioners tended to sit on every Sunday morning. Mostly, people stayed in one row or one section of the sanctuary as if they were planted there by God. I occupied those spaces and prayed for the congregants who belonged there. I even interceded for people who no longer attended the church. One man had been missing for a while, but when Dick got sick, the man sent me a card. In it, he explained that his brother had become ill with melanoma, and that he had been wondering what he could do to help me. His conclusion? He could be there for me. He started showing up again in church.

I will never again doubt the effectiveness of prayer or the importance of presence.

Chapter 22

DESPITE THE SUPPORT of a congregation or two, a pastor can grow weary. Sometimes the pastor wonders if he or she is making any difference at all. Sometimes a pastor just gets dry and feels empty. I know that is where I was when I started my journey on the road to Grace Place in Memphis, Tennessee. The activities of the previous few months had left me drained.

Billie and I met the Rev. Diane Harrison, founder of Grace Place, at a church growth clinic in Sikeston, Missouri. We were there to share stories about Calhoun and Drake's Chapel, and Diane was there to talk about her congregation of prison residents. The first thing I noticed about Diane was her joy, and the excitement she exuded about her prison ministry. Billie and I marveled at her unconventional congregation. We were lucky enough to sit at the same table with her. It was at that table that Billie and I began dreaming about going to Memphis and worshipping with the women at Grace Place.

As it turned out, things began to work out for a visit in 2015. Diane wasn't optimistic about us getting into the prison for worship, but we decided to go anyway and hope for the best. At least we would be able to spend some more time with Diane, we thought. She sent an email, cautioning us that it was going to take an Easter miracle to get us in.

The trip to Grace Place began with a beautiful, leisurely drive. Still, my mind raced. I kept thinking about how it would be once we were admitted. I wondered how it would feel to have the doors lock behind me. I was also concerned about how the women prisoners in the medium-security facility would feel about us. Would they accept us? Would they reject us?

As it turned out, our entrance into the Mark Luttrell Correctional Center was delayed. I had worn flip-flops. Prison rules prohibit flip-flops. I wasn't sure why the open-toed sandals were problematic, but it stated plainly on the wall that they were outlawed. A very kind woman took me down the street to a dollar store so that I could purchase an acceptable pair of shoes. Unfortunately, the only pair that fit my feet were a pair of canvas slip-ons, in a men's size 10. They were much too large for my feet (and, ironically, they flapped loosely as I walked in them), but the guards allowed me to wear them in even though I looked like a clown.

We made our way to the prison door. An alarm sounded and the bar gate opened. It shut behind us with a **bang!** We were trapped between that heavy gate and the next one. Another bell rang out, and the second gate opened automatically. We walked through it, only to see a *third* gate, with more bars. The sound of the second gate closing sent a chill down my spine. By the time the bell sounded once more and the third gate opened, I was ready to run in the other direction.

The chapel consisted of one room and a little closet. It was drab and had windows all around so that the guards could watch every move, even though none seemed overly interested in what was going on inside. The space really resembled a classroom, except for the altar in the middle of the floor. There was also a TV that someone had donated, so that the women could watch Bible study videos. My guess was that 25 inmates were present, along with a few volunteers and the two of us. We took our seats on the folding chairs and listened to Diane as she sat at the piano and began to play.

The choir started the service. Garbed in blue prison smocks and pants that resembled scrubs, the choir sang Crystal Lewis' "Come Just As You Are," which seemed fitting inasmuch as no one inside had the opportunity to change their status or appearance. What struck me, though, was the conviction with which the choir members belted out the invitational song. Like John Wesley, I felt my heart "strangely warmed," and tears flowed down my cheeks unashamedly.

Then it was time for the collection and, of course, no one had any money. The inmates offered thanks to God instead of offering envelopes. One prisoner after another expressed her gratitude: "for keeping me on the right path"; "for being with me through the night"; "for keeping my family safe"; "for knowing that I am not alone." One of the last speakers thanked God "for our guests who came all the way from Missouri." My tears reappeared as the women shared their gratitude.

Diane preached a powerful sermon, even though it was brief—an eight- or ten-minute sermonette, or a "word," as she called it. She took a passage from the New Testament and brought it to life. One of the young inmates moaned as she listened to the pastor's stirring message. Another woman shouted, "**Amen!**" several times when Diane made a point. Communion was equally moving. This was the first time that Billie had ever witnessed such an emotional exchange in church. As a new Christian from a small church in a small town, she was awestruck. It was beautiful. It was raw and real and it made us hungry to receive God's mercy and grace.

I believe Billie was deeply moved by her experience there at Grace Place. On the way home, we talked a mile a minute about what we had seen, heard and felt.

"They have nothing in our eyes," Billie concluded, "but, looking at them, I could tell that they have something that I want to possess."

How could I share our prison encounter with others and how could we help the ministry behind three steel gates? I wondered. My sermon the next Sunday described the Grace Place congregation—the worship experience, the remarkable choir composed of incarcerated women, the Inside Church Council and the way the women produced and sold handmade items to support mission projects. Crocheted crosses, angels, scarves and bears were all sold by Grace Place volunteers, as were copies of "A Taste of Grace Place" cookbook. The craft and cookbook sales meant that the church had been able to support a variety of organizations, such as Operation Smile (a nonprofit medical service organization), Mobility Worldwide (provider of personal energy transportation (PET) vehicles for individuals needing mobility), UMCOR (the United Methodist Committee on Relief) and FirstWorks (an after-school program for children).

I also mentioned that the women made the items they gave away, like hats and scarves for people experiencing homelessness and baby blankets and prayer shawls for those in the Methodist hospital. A few congregants also used plastic grocery bags to make sleeping mats for homeless people in Memphis.

"Surprised?" I asked rhetorically. "Don't be. Impactful mission is the result of passion and commitment, compassion and empathy. If these women can make such a tremendous difference without houses, cars, money or freedom, we need to support them and we need to follow their example."

Respond they did. Calhoun and Drake's Chapel sold Grace Place crafts at the fall festival, and then they decided to give their Christmas offerings to support the prison ministry. Over

$1,000 was donated. The two churches collected 300 toothbrushes for the women's facility, and a second trip to the prison was scheduled—and, this time, a third person joined Billie and me. After that, the Rev. Diane Harrison asked if she could personally thank my churches for all of their support. She preached in both places, challenging the churches to continue their outreach.

When I discovered that the women of Grace Place had watched all of the Rev. Adam Hamilton's Bible study videos, I contacted him and asked if he could record a short clip to encourage them the way they had encouraged us. In his kindness, he obliged. One of the women, Janell, was so taken by his message that she created a stunning crown of thorns using some empty biscuit boxes that she had salvaged from the mess hall. It was Adam's time to be awestruck.

On Palm Sunday, Adam used the thorny brown circlet as a sermon illustration at the Church of the Resurrection in Kansas. He explained that the crown was a gift from a prisoner and that it represented what God had done for her and the other women of Grace Place: redeeming what was considered trash and making it/them into something new and attractive. Adam told Janell's story and suggested that everyone in his congregation make a fresh start, too—as he hung her handsome crown on the cross.

Note: When the women's prison was relocated in 2016 to Henning, Tennessee—West Tennessee State Penitentiary Site 1—Grace Place moved with the prison.

Chapter 23

YEARS BEFORE I ever thought about being a lay minister in charge of two churches, in 1971 my husband and I moved with our 3-week-old son, Richard, to a small town of about 300 people, called Creighton. We didn't know a soul there. We chose the place because it was roughly halfway between Dick's work in Kansas City and our old hometown of Windsor, Missouri. We also selected it because it had a United Methodist church.

We got involved at the church right away. One thing we discovered almost immediately was that many of the people in the congregation were related to one another. It was a warm, friendly and family-like congregation, and soon we transferred our membership there. Next thing you know, we were asked to teach Sunday School and serve as United Methodist Youth sponsors.

Working with the children and youth was a handful for us. When debriefing on Sunday nights, Dick and I often wondered if we were making a difference at all. The kids had so much energy. They seemed more interested in games and mischief than in Jesus and God. Bobby was the prime example of a boy who challenged us. Every time I turned around, he was up to no good.

"Bobby, are you listening?" I'd ask. "Bobby, leave Julie alone." "Bobby, sit down." "Bobby, turn that tape player off."

With this history, I was caught off-guard when he confided, years later, that he felt God was calling him into the ministry. I laughed inside but outwardly, I responded by saying that if God wanted him to be a minister, then he would never be happy doing anything else. After he graduated from high school, one of his teachers told his parents not to waste their money. Nevertheless, Bobby went off to college with his high school sweetheart, Susan George. He graduated without any problems and was accepted into the Perkins School of Theology in Dallas, Texas.

I remember being in Texas for business and tacking on an extra day to my trip, so that I could worship at one of Bobby's student appointments. I couldn't get over what God had done in his life. Bobby read a challenging text before delivering a powerful, meaningful and passionate message. If buttons would have been on my heart that morning, they would have popped off from the pride I had in him. It's not that I take credit for the minister he had become; it's that I was a little responsible for him listening to the call of God and answering it.

He was ordained a deacon in 1983 and an elder in 1987. Bobby would go on to do great things for the Church. He planted Grace United Methodist Church in Lee's Summit in 1990, and Hope Church—a daughter congregation of Grace— in Lone Jack in 1998. While serving as senior pastor at the Church of the Shepherd in St. Charles, his congregation increased worship attendance from 450 to 1,200.

When Bobby was promoted to director of the conference's Center for Congregational Excellence, I started calling him Bob. It was in his role as conference director that he guided 35 church starts and oversaw 150 Healthy Church Initiative consultations. With Kay Kotan, he also authored several practical and popular books for clergy and laity, dealing with church growth and vitality.

During the second week of July in 2016, I was with Bob in Wichita, Kansas for the South Central Jurisdictional Conference of the United Methodist Church. There are five jurisdictions in the United States and every four years lay and clergy members of the annual conference are elected to attend the regional meetings. The jurisdictional conferences are where new bishops and members of the church's general board and agencies are elected.

Members of our conference's delegation had endorsed him as a candidate for bishop. He then was interviewed by other delegations as they considered who they would support. Finally, the delegates to Jurisdictional Conference voted. A percentage of the vote is required for someone to be elected. It was a highly charged meeting. The voting went on for two days. Bob was up one ballot and down the next. Finally, on the 35th vote, the convener made an announcement: "There has been an election. Bob Farr has been elected bishop!"

My eyes began to leak as I moved quickly down the aisle to congratulate him before he and his wife, Susan, were whisked to the front of the auditorium. He was busy receiving hugs and handshakes from everyone crowded around him. When he saw me in the mob, our eyes locked. He stopped, and gave me an embrace that I shall never forget. My ornery little boy had become an Episcopal leader. The teenager whose teacher determined that he wasn't right for college had been admitted to the United Methodist Council of Bishops.

Later that night, the Episcopal committee returned with the appointments of the new bishops. They had the responsibility of assigning bishops for Nebraska, Kansas, Arkansas, Texas and Louisiana, in addition to Missouri. God had one more shocker for me. Don House announced that the new bishop for Missouri was none other than Robert Dean Farr. The little mischievous boy would soon be my boss. He would supervise approximately 1,000 retired and active clergy, and oversee 800 local churches and 80,000 weekly worshippers.

Epilogue

IN A WORLD where bigger is usually perceived as better, Margie reminds us that small, strong churches have and still can play a vital role in people's spiritual lives. In *"Can You Just Get Them Through Until Christmas?"*, Margie helps us to see the possibilities: to see what a small, vibrant church is capable of achieving.

This is dear to my heart. I suspect that it is also dear to the hearts of many pastors and lay persons who grew up in small congregations across America. It saddens me to see so many of our small churches diminish to the point of no return. Demographics and cultural shifts have plotted against the small church as well as small-town America.

Many smaller communities have undergone systemic shifts in social status, ethnicity and economics. These towns and their churches have not been able to see the new possibilities and new people because they don't look like the things they have already done or the people they already know.

This book is full of ideas on how to reach people through small congregations and examples of how lives can be changed and transformed. Every small congregation could benefit from using Kay Kotan's study guide, at the back of the book, to explore some of the themes introduced in Margie's stories and to answer some of the questions posed about ministry, mission and outreach. You, your leaders and your whole church can explore this resource, praying to discern God's preferred future for your church as you begin a renewal process.

In the last 25 years, we have seen the closure of hundreds of churches. Some of this could not be helped or stopped, due to population decline and shifts. However, it is obvious—through Margie's experiences and many others like Margie's—that every small church does not have to die. Small churches can come alive—and have a great impact on people and their communities!

Unless we are going to give up on every town or village across the country with under 2,500 people, we need to figure out how to create, encourage and renew compelling and competent small churches, engaged in a ministry that is dedicated to reaching new people and doing whatever it takes.

Two key components are necessary in order for small churches to find new life and vitality:

- Lay leaders who are in love with Jesus, people and their mission field.
- A willingness on the part of the congregation. Where there is no willingness to change, all of the passion in the world on the part of the leadership cannot overcome the roadblocks of unwilling individuals. The unwillingness to change and try new things or engage different people overcomes any passion. When you get a passionate leader and a willing congregation, great ministry can happen.

It is my hope that these stories provide inspiration and hopefulness. It is my prayer that more and more small churches find new spirit and faithfulness.

I'm a product of small, faithful congregations from the 1970s. This type of congregation helped shape my life, as it did Margie's. It is my prayer that at least some of our rural churches can regain their vitality, so people there may once again be shaped and changed for the kingdom of God.

The church of yesterday is gone and is not coming back. Yet the church of tomorrow is beginning to step forth, with the power and anointment of God, when people leave behind their own preferences; their own wishes; their own agendas; and, instead, focus on the needs of others, for the sake of others and the kingdom of God. We need people who are willing, like Margie and others, to do whatever it takes to reach people they do not know and to strive for a future result they may not be able to see but reach for nonetheless, for the sake of Christ. This is what the lay circuit rider did in the early Methodist movement, and this is what we need to do again. We began as a lay pastor circuit rider movement, and we need to return to it, if our rural churches are to see the renewal that these communities so desperately need.

May it begin today.

—**Bishop Robert Farr**

Study Guide

by Kay Kotan

Chapter 1:

Key Concepts

- In an instant, everything can change.
- Sometimes in life, we are totally lost; our only option is to rely on God.
- When we have a human plan and not a God-given plan, God laughs.

Questions for Reflection

1. How can your church prepare people for major life changes—especially the unexpected ones?
2. Name a time when you felt totally lost. Describe your thoughts and feelings. How did God intersect during this time in your life?
3. What support systems to you have, personally, when bad things happen? What support systems are available for your congregation when bad things happen?

Chapter 2:

Key Concepts

- Ministers of all kinds (lay, local, deacons and elders) are just people with all of the same struggles as you and me.
- Each and every day is a blessing. Yet, we never know when a life-changing day is upon us.
- Death by suicide is different for the survivors.

Questions for Reflection

1. Even during this very difficult time, lay persons assumed leadership roles (i.e. looking for the pastor, making the announcement, leading prayer). In your church, is laity willing to lead if and when necessary?
2. The angel at the Drake's Chapel cemetery is an inspiring piece of wood carved from a dead tree. What are the features of your building and grounds that offer inspiring beauty and a sense of peace?
3. In offering your best to God, what maintenance and repairs have been neglected?

Chapter 3:

Key Concepts

- Grandparents can have a significant impact on the spiritual formation of their grandchildren, if given the chance.
- Spiritual habits formed at young ages can last a lifetime.
- United Methodists are part of a greater connection.

Questions for Reflection

1. Who was influential in your spiritual formation? How did they influence you? Who do you now have the opportunity to influence in their spiritual formation?

2. Name a time in the life of your congregation when the church, a family or an individual was "loved through" a situation or crisis. How did your congregation love them through it?

3. Granna offered a unique way of giving above and beyond the tithe. How does your congregation provide opportunities to grow in generosity in general? How do you, individually—and how does your church, collectively—grow in mission-giving?

Chapter 4:

Key Concepts

- Building relationships with new people takes time.
- We must build trust with people. Trust is earned, not given.
- Grieving is a process. It takes different pathways and different timeframes for each individual.

Questions for Reflection

1. God's timing and our timing is most often not the same. What is meant when one suggests God's timing is perfect?

2. Share a time when you or others have gone through the grieving process. Talk about the steps in the process.

3. Conflict or difficult times in churches can affect the life of a congregation for years, and sometimes decades, into the future. Name and discuss anything that your church might need to release, as it is the loving, grace-filled thing to do.

Chapter 5:

Key Concepts

- Each new pastor deserves a fresh start. Keep yourself and your church from comparing the new pastor to previous pastors.
- Just like everyone else, pastors sometimes feel ill-equipped for the ministry that God has called them into.
- The families of pastors are along for the ministry ride.

Questions for Reflection

1. Have you ever considered how the ministry of your pastor affects his or her family? Think about that for a moment. How might our expectations need some adjusting? How might we consider the price your minister's family pays in order for her or him to be in ministry?
2. We often think that our pastor comes to a new church with all the answers, training and confidence needed. Yet they are fully human. How is your church at seeing the gifts your pastor brings—and offering grace and support for their gaps?

3. Sometimes we believe a door has been closed, only to find that the closing was only temporary. Describe a time when you thought God had closed a door of opportunity, only for it to be opened in a wider way later.

Chapter 6:

Key Concepts

- Take advantage of forward momentum. Build on it!
- Believe that all things are possible through God.
- "Wins" build confidence. Confidence allows us to be more open to inviting others to be a part of the life of our congregation.

Questions for Reflection

1. What is possible for your church? What are your dreams for the future of your church?
2. What is holding you back?
3. Does your church have a legacy program in place that allows faithful members to remember the church at their passing?

Chapter 7:

Key Concepts

- Baptisms are a precious time for both the one being baptized and the congregation.
- Every time we witness a baptism, we are invited to remember our own baptism.
- Vital, small churches play a huge role in the kingdom of God.

Questions for Reflection

1. Reflect on your baptism. What do you remember about it (or what have you been told about it, if you were an infant)?
2. How does your church encourage and celebrate baptisms?
3. How many baptisms has your church had in the past year? The past decade? How do you feel about those numbers? What would you like to change in relation to baptisms?

Chapter 8:

Key Concepts

- God blesses us in and through brokenness.
- The church is not the building. The church is the people, and therefore worship can be wherever two or more are gathered.
- One part of being the church is loving and caring for fellow parishioners

Questions for Reflection

1. Reflect on a time when you felt personally broken. How did you once again feel whole?
2. Vital churches provide exceptional congregational care. How is your church at providing congregational care? If any improvements are needed, what are the steps necessary to improve your congregational care?

3. Name a small token that reminds you of God's grace and forgiveness. When and where did you acquire it? How does it remind you of God's grace and forgiveness?

Chapter 9:

Key Concepts

- A small-church pastor is the community pastor.
- The Holy Spirit leads us—especially at times when we are at a loss for words or actions.
- Ministers often offer pastoral care to individuals outside the congregation.

Questions for Reflection

1. Is the church's pastor seen as "your pastor" or the "community pastor"? Talk about what shifts might have to be made in order for him or her to move into a community model.
2. Recall a time when you were led by the Holy Spirit. Share your story with another. How has that Spirit-led experience affected your faith walk?
3. How does your congregation offer care for those outside the congregation in your community?

Chapter 10:

Key Concepts

- Poverty exists in almost all communities.
- It is important to know the needs of your community.

- It is important to not only meet the needs of your community, but also to offer relationship to your community.

Questions for Reflection

1. What is the greatest need in your community? How might your church be helpful in addressing that need?
2. Would anyone notice if you closed your doors tomorrow? Discuss who would and why.
3. How might the church also offer relationships (individually, as a congregation and with God) in addition to meeting community needs?

Chapter 11:

Key Concepts

- A small win for a small church can have a huge impact!
- Wins are many times achieved when we refuse to give up.
- Serving is as exhilarating as being served!

Questions for Reflection

1. Are you "going out" to bring children and other people into the church? Why or why not?
2. Name a "win" your church has achieved. How can you build on that win?

3. Sometimes congregants might declare that they can no longer serve due to a variety of reasons—or perhaps even excuses. Think about creative ways in which everyone can serve.

Chapter 12:

Key Concepts

- Church should be fun! Have a good time in church and doing church. Think bubbles and slippers!
- Creative worship keeps people engaged and guessing.
- Small churches have the opportunity to create even more intimate moments during worship.

Questions for Reflection

1. Would anyone dressed in any fashion be accepted at your church by everyone? Why or why not?
2. How is your church in praying to God about bringing in the people you need?
3. Describe the last time your church had fun in worship. How can you create fun moments more often?

Chapter 13:

Key Concepts

- A small church can have a huge impact both on a local as well as a national scale, doing seemingly smaller things.
- One never knows the impact of his or her ministry now or in the future.

- All churches need inspiration, but small churches certainly need to see vibrant ministry being done in smaller, rural congregations.

Questions for Reflection

1. How is your church impacting your community and beyond?
2. Describe a time when you had no idea, at the time, that a ministry was making an impact. What could be learned from that experience?
3. How can your church either provide inspiration or gain inspiration from other small churches? What steps will allow this to happen?

Chapter 14:

Key Concepts

- Churches have the opportunity to be an integral part of the community, especially when it comes to events that are decades in the making.
- Community events offer the opportunity to raise both awareness and funds for people in the community with special needs (i.e. a child's critical illness).
- Having fun together as a church is great for the congregation, as participants, but also for the community, as witnesses. Being a part of a church can be fun!

Questions for Reflection

1. What are the staple, big events in your community? How does your church support and participate in these activities?

2. Describe a time when your church supported a community member in need through a community effort. How does your church keep an eye out for other future opportunities?
3. How does your church play together? How does your church invite the community to play together and have fun, too?

Chapter 15:

Key Concepts

- Planting seeds for future "watering" and "fertilizing" (potentially by others) is part of being the church.
- Understanding the gaps and listening closely to the needs of your community—as well as how to fill them—is part of being in ministry for your community.
- Focusing on new people hearing the Good News is not only our responsibility as Christians and the church; it is our joy and our blessing.

Questions for Reflection

1. How is your church planting "God seeds" in the community? How might there be an opportunity to plant more seeds?
2. What opportunities to meet people's needs in your community—beyond the basics (food, shelter, clothing)—could you build on by empowering people and bringing them joy?

3. How is your church doing good deeds while sharing the Good News? How are you collecting names and following up with a relational connection process?

Chapter 16:

Key Concepts

- Mission trips are about the relationships as much or more so than the labor.
- Mission trips offer opportunities for us to gain new experiences and think beyond our local communities.
- People often decide to participate in mission trips for the opportunity to make a difference or transform another community, but many times, God provides them with an internal transformation.

Questions for Reflection

1. What mission opportunities is your church providing for its members—of *all* ages?
2. Describe your last mission trip experience. Where did you go? What did you do? How did it affect your spiritual journey?
3. How might a mission trip offer a wider understanding of the world that might not be experienced in another venue?

Chapter 17:

Key Concepts

- Fellow congregants "circle up" in times of need.
- The blessings received in serving are far greater than those given.
- Many times, God calls us outside our comfort zones in ministry—for growth, and to flex our ministry muscles.

Questions for Reflection

1. Describe a time when your congregation has "circled up" around a person in their final days. What did you learn in those times? What was the heartache? What was the blessing?
2. Share a story of a time when God provided people to minister to you in your time of need. How did this affect your faith journey?
3. What is the process in your church that allows you to be finely tuned into people: to meet their needs in their final days?

Chapter 18:

Key Concepts

- Practicing spiritual disciplines is important for spiritual growth.
- Communion is particularly meaningful and impactful for many.
- Thinking beyond the church walls to offer prayer and communion is an important part of ministry to consider.

1. What spiritual disciplines do you practice regularly?
2. What spiritual disciplines would you like to practice on a more regular basis?
3. Describe a memorable communion experience. What made it memorable?

Chapter 19:

Key Concepts

- Providing recognition and support for community servants is an important part of ministry.
- Churches need to concentrate on what they *can* do rather than on what they can't or used to do.
- Small community gestures can have a huge impact. Schools are the absolute best community partners. Make sure that building relationships with the students and faculty is deemed a priority, in addition to providing resources.

Questions for Reflection

1. How can your church provide needed recognition and appreciation for community servants?
2. Who, in your community, has been overlooked while providing tireless service to the community?
3. What is your church known for in your community?

Chapter 20:

Key Concepts

- All are worthy of and invited for baptism.
- Laity are called into ministry, too.
- The Holy Spirit guides us into some of the most amazing ministry opportunities, if only we are willing to follow.
- Trust your gut feelings. They are not indigestion. What you are feeling is God working through you.

Questions for Reflection

1. Describe a time when you responded to a moving of the Holy Spirit; when you did not respond. Talk about the differences between those two experiences.
2. How would you talk to someone about their feelings of unworthiness for baptism?
3. How is your church intentionally reaching out to both the unchurched and dechurched people in your community?

Chapter 21:

Key Concepts

- Sometimes a congregation needs to provide pastoral care for its minister.
- Non-anxious presence is important during high-need times.
- Different people may take on different roles, depending on who is needing the ministering and who is available at the time.

Questions for Reflection

1. When might your pastor need ministering? How does your congregation remain vigilant in noticing when it is needed—and providing it?
2. How is prayer a part of an impending death or critical illness?
3. In critical times, what role do your spiritual gifts normally allow you to fill? Explain.

Chapter 22:

Key Concepts

- Ministry and life can sometimes be draining. We need to fill our cups routinely.
- Cup-filling sometimes happens in unusual ways.
- Seeing others' gratitude in less-than-ideal circumstances often puts our own blessings into perspective.

Questions for Reflection

1. How to you gain spiritual renewal when your cup is low or dry?
2. How does your congregation offer opportunities for the pastor's spiritual renewal?
3. How do you recognize and celebrate your blessings with gratitude?

Chapter 23:

Key Concepts

- God can make things happen far beyond what we think possible.
- Dream big! God can dream even bigger!
- One never knows what seeds he or she is planting.

Questions for Reflection

1. If your church expects to receive a pastor, what is the congregation doing to "raise up" and inspire potential future pastors (and bishops)?
2. How are you pouring into the next generation, with a goal of "raising up" future church leaders and pastors?
3. Who has God placed on your heart who might need some encouragement and support in recognizing his or her ministry gifts (whether for clergy or laity)?

Margie's List of 10 Top Rut Busters

IS YOUR CHURCH stuck in a rut? If so, try one or more of these rut busters that helped our churches climb out of that trench!

1. Walk around your community and survey it with new eyes. Pray for your community and listen for God's answers. How can you be God's hands and feet in your community?

2. Connect with local schools. See what you can do to help the children in your area. (We hold a back-to-school event. It involves a free breakfast, free haircuts and the distribution of school supplies and hygiene items.)

3. Host a luncheon for the teachers and administrators from the community schools, to thank them for their work with the community's children.

4. Recruit a mission team to join you as you work in the neighborhood. (We picked people and places not connected with the church for mission activities.)

5. Initiate or reinstate a baccalaureate service for graduates and their families. (We host a sit-down dinner before the event, to make it a special evening.)

6. Host a "Jesus' birthday party" to introduce the community children to the real reason for Christmas. (The first year, we had to gather kids off the street for this. Today, the party's reputation has grown and people approach us to participate. Also, the Christmas Store has expanded so as to allow everyone in the family a chance to shop for free.)

7. Plan a fundraiser for a person or family from the neighborhood who needs help. (We once raised money to rehab a family's house whose daughter was the victim of a horrific accident.)

8. Establish a food ministry. (Our food pantry is open on the last Friday of every month. Since we are assisting people who are employed, but also poor, it is open after working hours.)

9. Start an appreciation event for first responders: EMTs, firefighters and/or police officers. (We hold a dinner and present the rescuers with a certificate of appreciation and a picture of the station.)

10. Have an annual, community-wide Easter egg hunt during which the story of Easter is shared in different ways. (We give away prizes to all of the children.)

Acknowledgments

THIS IS MY feeble attempt to thank the many individuals who have stood by me on my journey to this point in my life as I have tried to make a small difference in my world:

I first must acknowledge my grandmother Lutjen for her devotion to teach me and show me that there are not limits to God's love for me. Her wise words and actions taught me I would always have enough time and money to do the things that were important to me, but I must use both very carefully.

To all the United Methodist churches of which I have been a member: Windsor, Belton, and Creighton as well as the members of those churches. The congregations encouraged me and helped me become a leader.

The United Methodist Women who have played a huge role in who I am today.

This book would never have come to be if it had not been for these people who stood by me and became my cheerleaders.

My dear friend, and publisher, Rev. Faith Fowler, who believed I had a story to tell and gently pushed me to make it happen.

Kay Kotan, author and friend, who helped me to see I could write a book and stepped up to help it become a reality.

My former District Superintendent, Rev. Dr. Cody Collier, who encouraged me for years to write a book which would share the stories of my two amazing churches with a much wider circle. Cody baptized many at my churches and was the one who articulated the words, "Can you just get them through until Christmas." His 30+ year friendship and belief in me has been a priceless gift.

The women Bishops of the United Methodist Church, especially, Bishop Ann Sherer-Simpson, Bishop Janice Huie, Bishop Beverly Shamana, Bishop Mary Ann Swenson, Bishop Jane Ann Middleton, Bishop Deb Keisey, Bishop Violet Fisher, and Bishop Leontine T. Kelly, whom I have the pleasure of working with. These brave women gave me more than they can ever know and have shown little girls all over this country that God indeed calls women to serve God.

The women pastors in my life have played a huge part in my answering God's call. My thanks and love to: Rev. Marie Hyatt, Rev. Barbara Bowser, Rev. Sally Haynes, Rev. Amy Turner, Rev. Jan Bond, Rev. Lynn Dyke, Rev. Sherry Habben, Rev. Michele Sue Shumake-Keller, Rev. Sandy Nenadal, Rev. Dorothy Smith, Rev. Robin Roderick, and Rev. Nora Jones.

The two churches I serve, Calhoun United Methodist and Drake's Chapel United Methodist Church, I am not sure I have adequate words to express my thanks to all of you. You accepted me as the person I was and because of your love and support, I have become who I am today. You were willing to try anything I came up with, and you did it with joy. You didn't care that my only degree was in life itself. You were okay with others coming to baptize those who said yes to Jesus. You welcomed all who walked through the doors and ministered to those outside the doors and invited them in.

To Bishop Farr, Rev. Adam Hamilton and Rev. Dianne Harrison—giants in the kingdom—I am grateful you have allowed me to include your inspiring stories.

To some other special people (You know who you are) who have picked me up when I was down and danced with me on mountain tops during my life: Your laughter and tears are a precious gift.

To my dearest friend and Savior, Jesus Christ. Thank you for leading me on a path I was unsure of, yet ready to follow because I was sure you knew the way. I pray these stories will be an instrument to encourage small rural churches to continue bringing the Gospel in their communities, and for lay people to listen for God's call on their lives. Don't be fearful of following a pathway presently unknown.

Photo Captions

Chapter One: Margie at her desk during the IXC days when she was only 17 miles from their home in Creighton.

Chapter Two: The angel, carved from a white oak tree, stands in the cemetery across the road from Drake's Chapel.

Chapter Three: Margie's former District Superintendent, mentor, and friend, Rev. Dr. Cody Collier with five of her grandchildren in the front of the Calhoun sanctuary.

Church Four: A beautiful sunset from the front porch at the Briggs' farm.

Chapter Five: A photo of the appointments/assignments for pastors distributed at the Annual Conference. Margie took the shot using a cell phone camera to tell her church people that she was coming back.

Chapter Six: Workers install a new roof at Calhoun, thanks to Roland Hess and his roofing company.

Chapter Seven: This is one of the beautiful new stained glass windows at Calhoun. The dark haired angel with the lion and lamb is in memory of Melody Dorris. Her youngest daughter takes care of the church's media needs and will be married in the church in July 2017.

Chapter Eight:
TOP - Vennie and Dale bring a new freezer of homemade ice cream out for the ice cream social at Drake.
BOTTOM – Margie holds the broken chalice during the outdoor worship service at Bill and Marsha's timber.

Chapter Nine: A trip to Kansas City to take items to Grand Ave. Temple UMC always ends in some fun for the youth group. This time ice skating at Crown Center.

Chapter Ten: One wall of Calhoun food pantry, that brings help and hope to the community on the 4th Friday of the month.

Chapter Eleven: This picture shows a later Vacation Bible School when the crowd was a little larger than the first one.

Chapter Twelve: The year Margie told the resurrection story from Mary's perspective.

Chapter Thirteen: Rev. Adam Hamilton, a friend for many years, at his church, Church of the Resurrection in Leawood, Kansas.

Chapter Fourteen:
TOP - A sign welcomes people to Calhoun.
BOTTOM - A parade float from Drake's Chapel.

Chapter Fifteen: Children come to the Welcome Room at the Calhoun Church to choose gifts from the tables' heavy laden with Easter prizes.

Chapter Sixteen:
TOP - The Detroit group that rocked Calhoun when they came to town to do mission work with us.
BOTTOM - The group from Calhoun at the Heidelberg Project in Detroit, Michigan.

Chapter Seventeen: Left to right - Billie, me, Pearl and Rai at the celebration of our beloved friend Georgia's life.

Chapter Eighteen: My friends Josephine, and her daughter, Grace after a 1st Sunday visit and sharing Communion.

Chapter Nineteen: The Calhoun basement jammed full with teachers and staff for the "Back to School Lunch" the day before school year started.

Chapter Twenty: Dale and Sharon Miller on a good day. Sharon is now a member of the Calhoun Church.

Chapter Twenty-One: Dick and Margie on their 25th wedding anniversary.

Chapter Twenty-Two: The crown of thorns made out of trash by a member of Grace Place.

Chapter Twenty-Three: Bishop Robert D. Farr back when his job was mowing yards in Creighton, and Margie called him Bobby.

The Epilogue: Margie addressed the Annual Conference after receiving the Harry Denman Evangelism Award in 2010.

Rut Busters: Margie in her women in ministry t-shirt (showing a woman with her hair in a bun, a book in her hands and riding on a horse superimposed over the state of Missouri). The casual top celebrated 60 years of full ordination rights of women and was created by Rev. Laura Blevins.

About the Author

MARGIE LUTJEN BRIGGS was born in Windsor, Missouri. She graduated from Windsor High School in 1966, and married Dick Briggs while still in high school. Together, Margie and Dick raised three children: Richard, Heather and Taylor. Margie is a grandmother of nine.

As a layperson, Margie was active in the Creighton United Methodist Church and in United Methodist Women (UMW), a faith-based membership organization of laywomen in the United Methodist Church. Serving as district president of the UMW and dean of the Missouri School of Christian Mission, Margie was later asked to pastor both Drake's Chapel United Methodist Church and Calhoun United Methodist Church. She was elected to attend General Conference seven times (between 1992 and 2016). Margie served as a board member for the General Commission on the Status and Role of Women from 1996 to 2004, and on the General Board of Church and Society from 1996 to 2012.

Margie became a certified lay minister in 2008. In 2010, she was the recipient of the Harry Denman Evangelism Award and the John Bennett Award for Excellence in Rural Ministry.

About the Study Guide Author

KAY L. KOTAN is a credentialed coach, church consultant and speaker. She has authored and co-authored numerous books. Several books were written with Bishop Robert Farr and published by Abingdon Press: *Renovate or Die: 10 Ways to Focus Your Church on Mission* (2011), *Get Their Name: Grow Your Church by Building New Relationships* (2013), *10 Prescriptions for a Healthy Church* (2015) and *The Necessary Nine* (2016).

Other books include *Insights on Productivity, Ministry 3.0, Full Schedules, Barren Souls* and *Strategic Ministry Planning*.

Her most recent books are *Gear Up!* (2017), *Mission Possible* (2017) and *Building Worship Bridges* (2017).

CPSIA information can be obtained
at www.ICGtesting.com
Printed in the USA
LVHW01s1704110118
562654LV00004B/19/P